START YOUR OWN
TELEMARKETING
BUSINESS

START YOUR OWN
TELEMARKETING
BUSINESS

Extra Income Magazine
National Business Library

Scott, Foresman and Company
Glenview, Illinois   London

ISBN 0-673-46339-7

1 2 3 4 5 6 RRC 95 94 93 92 91 90

Library of Congress Cataloging in Publication Data

Start Your Own Telemarketing Business / National Business
Library.
    p.   cm.
    Includes bibliographical references.
    ISBN 0-673-46339-7
    1. Telemarketing. 2. New business enterprises. I. National
    Business Library.
HF5415.1265.S73 1990
658.8'4—dc20   90–8084
                                             CIP

Scott, Foresman Professional Books Group books are available for
bulk sales at quantity discounts. For more information, please contact
Marketing Manager, Professional Books, M–300, Professional Books
Group, Scott, Foresman and Company, 1900 E. Lake Avenue,
Glenview, Il 60025.

Dear Friend,

I would personally like to extend my congratulations to you on taking the first all-important step in making your dream of owning your own business a reality.

Start Your Own Telemarketing Business is the result of many hours of in-depth research into the Telemarketing industry. Our exclusive team of professional business writers have brought years of practical experience to this project and we know that the information provided in this book will set you on the road to success.

Owning your own business can be the most exciting and rewarding venture you will ever experience. We talk to hundreds of small business owners who make comments like, "Doing something I really enjoy makes every new day a pleasure," or "If I had known I could be realizing this kind of income, rather than making my former boss wealthy, I would have started my own business years ago."

It's true! You'll never get rich working for someone else. By capitalizing on your experience, investing time and energy, and studying the proven techniques and business methods provided in this book, you will be well on the way to realizing your goals for success in your own venture. It takes courage to begin. Without a doubt, the first step is the hardest—and you have already taken it!

Sincerely,

James J. Maher
Publisher

P.S. Please let me know when you have established your new business. I look forward to congratulating you again! If yours is an interesting or unique new business story, we may include it in our series as we have done for hundreds of others.

Acknowledgments

The project editor on this book was Diane Beausoleil. The cover was designed by Interface Studio, and the text design was developed by BMR, Inc. Lisa Labrecque was project manager. The book was made into pages by BMR using Pagemaker 3 on the Macintosh. The text type is Palatino and Helvetica condensed. The entire project was coordinated by Gene Schwartz of Consortium House, Ltd., Del Mar, California. This book was printed and bound by R. R. Donnelley.

Start Your Own
Telemarketing Business
Table of Contents

INTRODUCTION

Telemarketing Service Bureau:
Turn Your Telephone into a "Gold Line"

Possibly the most exciting business opportunity of the coming decade, telemarketing has taken the country by storm. In less than ten years, sales resulting from the telemarketing industry have reached the $100 billion mark—and that's just the tip of the iceberg, according to business experts who are predicting the same kind of action over the next *three* years. And, *Business Week* magazine estimates that by the year 2000, there will be more than eight million jobs just in telemarketing alone!

If you have the ability to be convincing over the telephone, enjoy communicating with people, and are self-motivated, there is plenty of room in this extremely profitable business. Whether your long-range goals are to earn a little extra income handling one or two small business accounts or to realize some big bucks operating your own telemarketing service bureau with major corporations as clients, telemarketing offers a solid opportunity.

The profit potential in this business is limited only by your ability and willingness to work. The choice is yours — $500 to $1,000 a month making appointments for local insurance agents or $5,000 a month selling products by telephone for big companies— which is another aspect that makes this business so attractive. You call the shots and can basically dictate the amount of money you make! So read on for details on how you can start your own telemarketing service bureau and be dialing for dollars in the very near future! ∎

1

The Growth of Small Business

The 1980s have been referred to as America's "entrepreneurial era." In 1985, there were 500,000 new business start-ups in this country, but in the following year that number increased to an incredible 750,000. Last year, more than one million new businesses were started in this country—with almost half by women—and this figure is expected to rise dramatically during the early 1990s.

More and more people are opting to leave their 9-to-5 jobs and stop "making someone else rich" to focus their energies on building a successful business of their own. For these people, it is no longer enough to spend nearly three-quarters of their lives working in a dead-end job, putting up with petty office politics, unappreciative employers and wasting time on long commutes just to bring home headaches and a small paycheck.

You can never be too young,
too old, too busy or too poor to
start a business.

Today, the number of individuals who are self-employed is at its highest level ever and, based on your decision to study this business guide, it is quite possible that you will be joining the ranks of small business owners in the near future. It may be simply a dream at this moment, but that is how it starts.

Starting and operating your own small business is one of the most exciting and satisfying challenges you can undertake. There are no limitations on income potential when you are investing time and energy in your own enterprise. With the practical information provided in this guide and dedication to your business goals, your chances for success are excellent.

What *is* a "Small Business"?

The majority of businesses in the U.S. today are classified as small businesses. The definitions of what constitutes a small business run the gamut from fewer than 500 employees to various indicators of annual assets or sales volumes. However, in this book, small business is defined as one which is independently owned and operated.

The major benefit of this type of business is that you have the ability to make decisions quickly and act on them immediately; something that typically bogs down big businesses because of the number of people involved in the decision-making process. The other advantages include the fact that small businesses can provide personalized service to the community or the market they are serving and that the owner has the freedom, the independence and the control to operate exactly as he or she chooses.

It is still important to remember, however, that most major corporations, from Ford Motor Company and McDonald's to Mary Kay Cosmetics, started out as small businesses, as dreams. It was because of basic business sense and a willingness to learn and adapt as their companies grew that Henry Ford, Ray Kroc and Mary Kay, and thousands like them, steered their dreams into monumental financial successes.

Whether your goal is to operate a solely owned home-based business from your garage, the kitchen table, or a spare bedroom that supplements an existing income, or to start a business venture that involves raising substantial capital, finding and setting up a commercial location and hiring employees, you have the potential to enjoy an independent lifestyle that carries with it a number of rewards.

Entrepreneur

A person who undertakes an independent enterprise; one who has made the decision to go into business for him/herself.

Accepting the Challenge

However, these rewards do not come without hard work and the willingness to research and understand all facets of running your business. Many new businesses fail within the first few years.

Reasons given for the early demise of a small business invariably include comments from the owners pertaining to undercapitalization, misunderstanding of the importance of advertising, confusion about pricing products or services and a lack of knowledge in areas of financial planning and day-to-day operating techniques.

It isn't that someone purposely starts a business without having explored these areas. However, many times a person feels that because they have been a good woodworker, computer operator, salesperson, or any other specialist, while working for someone else, they can easily transfer their expertise into their own business. This is only partially true.

While it is imperative that you have these certain skills or talents—because selling them is what your ultimate success will be based upon—it is equally important to understand *how* to sell them, how to recognize whether you are *really* making money or not, and what steps to take to ensure the continued growth of your business.

Sounds easy, right? It really can be. But like anything else worth doing, starting your own business means careful planning. You wouldn't consider taking a month-long vacation without doing some serious planning to ensure that the house was taken care of while you were gone, that you had made reservations for lodging, tours and flights, and converted your cash into traveler's checks, etc.

There are so many aspects involved with running a business, it is vital to be prepared for any eventuality, and being prepared comes, quite simply, from being informed, so that when situations do arise, you know how to deal with them.

Is "Failure" Really Failure?

We have all heard stories about people who started their businesses on a "shoestring" with little more than a wing and a prayer and were successful because of their sheer determination to make it work. It does happen, but these people are the exception rather than the rule, and in most cases have had experts standing behind them to give them guidance when problems come up. Others do fail and, unfortunately, this is a factor that often holds potential new business owners back. We hear and read amazingly high figures related to business failure.

A recent survey conducted by a New York-based business consulting firm indicated that many people, including small business owners, believe that up to ninety percent of all new companies fail within their first year. This is simply not true.

According to an on-going research project conducted by Albert Shapero, Professor of the American Free Enterprise System at Ohio State University for many years, no one really knows the true failure rate of new business. The main reason for this is because there is not really a standard definition of "failure" in this case. He points out that a number of businesses close for a variety of reasons that are rarely documented.

For example, in some cases the owners reach retirement age and have no one to pass the business along to; others shut down because the owners simply get bored; while some entrepreneurs will file a Chapter 11 bankruptcy, which basically gives them the opportunity to stay in business and continue operating under a court-approved plan even though they become a statistic on the "failure" list.

The other extremely important aspect to consider when thinking about the benefits and risks of starting your own business is that having a business fail has never been a deterrent for true entrepreneurs. Many well-known business moguls failed at least once, and often more than once, before striking it rich.

Learning from Experience

In fact, almost anyone who has had a business fail will tell you that what they learned from the experience was more valuable than anything they could have been taught in a business school, and provided them with the knowledge they needed to start another venture successfully. This kind of determination is a valid qualification for self-employment and will certainly pay off handsomely.

When you own your own business, you are generally chief cook and bottle-washer. There will be times, such as when your accounts receivables are running 60 days late, or the phone company puts the wrong number in your Yellow Page listing, when returning to the world of 9-to-5 will seem like a viable option.

This is where self-discipline, an unwavering belief in your product or service, and the determination to be your own boss will pull you through. But, again, we can't stress enough the importance of planning, understanding basic business practices, being aware of consumer trends, and taking the time to develop, implement, and update goals to ensure success for your efforts.

Inside this Book

This book is designed to provide you with the information you will need to start your telemarketing service bureau, techniques to help you with day-to-day operations, and actual case histories of people just like you who had a dream and, through planning and determination, were able to turn it into a successful reality.

In addition to focusing on aspects of the telemarketing business, we cover important business matters ranging from the entrepreneurial profile and our exclusive Entrepreneurial Quiz, how to find the right audience for your business through easy marketing techniques and organizing for efficiency, to legalities, financial concerns, the ease with which you can establish your telemarketing business at home while you get it up and running, and methods for charting growth.

You will find specific how-to information on advertising and promoting your business, finding capital, saving money on operating expenses, and developing a simple bookkeeping system that will show you, at a glance, whether you are facing a financial crisis or realizing a profit.

You're never too young, too old, too busy or too poor to start a business. Owning your own business means taking advantage of our marvelous system of free enterprise. Earning a substantial living and, even better, realizing a profit for doing something you enjoy is the American dream come true.

The road to financial independence through self-employment is challenging and rewarding. The opportunities for entrepreneurs have never been better. Armed with a solid product or service to sell, the determination to succeed and, most important, business know-how, there is nothing that can stand in your way. ■

Notes

Key Points

_____

_____

_____

_____

Personal Thoughts

_____

_____

_____

_____

_____

_____

Additional Research

_____

_____

_____

_____

_____

2

The Entrepreneurial Profile

Starting a business is one thing; making it work is another. Success in self-employment is largely the result of careful planning and the understanding of basic business techniques and formulas.

Start a business based on your expertise in a specific field and focus your involvement in an area that you thoroughly enjoy. As many successful entrepreneurs claim, making money doing something you love is the best way to ensure a profitable future. Addressing inevitable business challenges with creating a product or providing a service is easier when it gives you a sense of pleasure and personal satisfaction.

Personality is also a factor in determining what kind of business to get involved in, the way you will eventually set up the legal structure (sole proprietorship, partnership, etc.) and how you will run the business on a day-to-day basis. For example, if you are planning to start a business which is based on your artistic or creative abilities, it is possible that your personality is not suited to the very important aspect of sales. But without strong selling abilities there is a likelihood that your goal of distributing nationally, for example, your hand-carved wooden boxes will not come to fruition.

This is not to say that you should decide against going into business for yourself. It simply indicates that it would be in your best interest to join forces with someone who *does* have strong selling skills, who believes in the product as much as you do and will work toward a common goal.

On the other hand, if your personality is geared to working with people, consider a business that will emphasis this ability, such as developing seminars or workshops based on your area of expertise, providing independent counseling or tutoring, or a service such as desktop publishing, which depends on your interaction with people on a one-to-one or a group basis for success.

Ten Positive Entrepreneurial Traits

1. Motivation	6. Optimism
2. Confidence	7. Experience
3. Self-awareness	8. Decisiveness
4. Courage	9. Patience
5. Knowledge	10. Drive

Self-motivation, otherwise known as drive, is one of the most important personality traits of successful entrepreneurs. This is the characteristic that gets you going and keeps you moving when you are in business for yourself. It's what helps you to keep turning out those wooden boxes, upgrading your technical skills or develop new and improved promotional techniques when business is slow. It's what gives you the tenacity and confidence to call on a potential client even though they have told you 'No' three times.

Self-motivation is also what helps you to overcome the fears and concerns that inevitably arise when you own your own business. It is the main ingredient which has spurred on those people we hear about who have achieved success despite drawbacks, such as minimal capital, lack of education, or limited experience.

People with a high degree of self-motivation see the greatest obstacles, such as learning a new aspect of business management, as new and exciting challenges to be overcome. If you have ever undertaken a project without fully understanding the mechanics involved in performing the task or knowing what the outcome would be, you were operating on self-motivation—the conviction that you would be able to learn whatever was needed to accomplish your goal.

And regardless of the outcome of the project, you undoubtedly gained more experience and knowledge than you had before, which only works to increase your sense of motivation to handle new challenges.

Research shows that to be able to address the many and varied situations that arise in business ownership, the true entrepreneur should possess the following kinds of personality traits:

The willingness to take risks. Courage is a valuable trait when striving for success. We have heard successful people say something similar to this, "I don't know how I did it, I just made a phone call and asked for the money I needed." It was more than luck that made it possible for this person to raise the capital they needed to get their business off the ground; it was the willingness to take a chance—in this case, the risk that they would receive a negative response to the request.

The owner of a small cabinet-refinishing business said, "I always figure that the worst thing that can happen is someone will say no, so it never hurts to try." In the game of business, you must be willing to take chances. Even if you don't get exactly what you want every time, the odds are good that if you feel strongly about what you need, you will get it. But you have to ask!

Confidence. The age-old philosophy of positive thinking is a step in the direction of success. By behaving as if you already are a success at what you do, it follows that you will be, and your customers will believe it, too. A confident attitude is one of the most appealing traits you can exhibit to a prospective client, for it lets them know that they will be getting the best their money can buy.

Patience. When you own your own business, there will be moments when you feel like the roof is caving in, especially when your suppliers seem to be taking their own sweet time in fulfilling an important order, or when a customer's demands seem to be unrealistic. Although you may be able to hurry the supplier along a little bit, you must remember that your customers are always right, since they are the ones who can financially make or break your business.

If you are aware that patience is not your strong suit, develop a stop-gap exercise for yourself to use at times when coping is a definite necessity. Whether it's the time-honored 'count to ten before saying a word' theory, visualizing a pleasant scene, or repeating a secret phrase to yourself when tension is running high, it will be to your advantage.

You have to accept whatever comes,
and the important thing is
that you meet it with courage
and with the best you have to give.

Eleanor Roosevelt

Decision-making. Business has been described as a process of one decision after another. Often, a decision has to be made on the spur-of-the-moment. In those instances, you should go with your intuition and trust that you are doing the right thing.

However, if you are the type of person who prefers to analyze your options, weigh all the factors and make decisions slowly, then this is what you must do. It will not only keep your confidence intact, but will ensure that you are taking the correct action. Again, careful planning will help you predict many of the decision-making situations that arise in business. As time goes by and you grow more comfortable in your role as business owner, you will undoubtedly find yourself making decisions more quickly.

Experience.   The results of a Dun & Bradstreet survey conducted a few years back indicated that a primary reason that some businesses fail within a few years after start-up was 'incompetence in the area of business experience.' Whether or not your experience is directly related to the business you are planning to start, it is an essential component for growth.

If you feel you do not have enough business experience, there are several avenues you can take before starting your own enterprise. Returning to school for specialized courses is one answer. Most community colleges and adult education facilities offer classes and seminars in business start-up and maintenance. There are also hundreds of courses available to you by mail—over 1,200 schools and universities now offer home study or correspondence courses which will, in many cases, give you official certification in your field.

However, your best solution is to take a job in the field you are interested in. By asking questions about all aspects of the business, you will gain experience, be getting paid for learning, and find out whether this is really what you want to do—before sinking money, time, and energy into the enterprise.

Perseverance.   One of the adages you will hear time and time again when talking to entrepreneurs is that perseverance is ninety percent of the battle to succeed. If you are like the majority of new small business owners, the entire staff and support system for your venture is probably *you*. Making a dream come true can be a lonely task, especially when you are just getting started, and ensuring that it works often means little rest and relaxation. You must be willing to persevere during the rough times, to hang in there during the slow periods, and to maintain your belief in your product and service even when it seems like no one else in the world knows you exist. It has been written that by perseverance, the snail reached the ark. So it is with success!

The Entrepreneurial "A to Z" Appraisal

Owning a business calls for the ability to handle many different situations with confidence. The following self-appraisal quiz has no right or wrong answers. It is designed to help you in determining personality traits, attitudes and qualifications which will benefit you in your venture.

Use the letters "S" for strong or "N" for needs improvement beside the characteristics listed below. Give yourself sufficient time to analyze each trait. Upon completion, use the appraisal as a starting point for discussions with friends and family members about your business profile. Acknowledging your strong and weak points will help you prepare for your role as an entrepreneur.

Achievement. I have a strong desire to be successful in my chosen business venture. _____

Belief. I have faith in myself and the service or product I am specializing in to build my business. _____

Creativity. I am able to address situations in imaginative and innovative ways to reach my goals. _____

Discipline. I am self-motivated and able to handle necessary tasks, whether or not I enjoy them. _____

Efficient. I am organized and able to arrange my priorities or change my work methods as needed for maximum production. _____

Friendly. I am genuinely interested in people and enjoy my interactions with them on a day-to-day basis. _____

Goal-oriented. I have a tendency to set my sights on pre-set goals and to work hard toward them. _____

Health-conscious. I am aware of my physical abilities and have the insight to work smart in order to preserve my health. _____

Independent. I am able to work alone, if necessary, and prefer to be responsible for my own actions. _____

Judgment. My conclusions about people or situations are generally accurate. _____

Knowledge. I have solid experience in my field and have spent enough time in a professional business setting to learn the ropes. _____

Leadership. I am able to direct people effectively while instilling confidence and loyalty. _____

Maturity. I am willing to work toward long-term goals and do not get upset by the inevitable minor set-backs. _____

Networking. I have, or am willing to develop, associations with other entrepreneurs for support in my venture. _____

Optimism. I am able to see what is right about a situation and to explore its potential to the fullest. _____

Positive attitude. I am convinced that I can accomplish anything I set my mind to doing and rarely entertain negative thoughts. _____

Questioning. I am not afraid to ask questions to get the information I need to expand my knowledge. _____

Resourceful. I am able to find ways to accomplish just about any task I must do. _____

Sales ability. I can present information about my-self and my business in a convincing and honest manner.   _____

Tolerance. I am able to handle stressful situations with a positive and realistic attitude.   _____

Undaunted spirit. I am unafraid of the unknown. In fact, I enjoy a challenge and accept the consequences of my actions.   _____

Venturesome. I am not afraid of hard work to reach my goals and enjoy finding new, positive ways to handle troublesome situations.   _____

Well-balanced. I generally maintain a sense of humor when things don't work out as expected.   _____

eXpressive. I am able to express ideas and feelings, both orally and in writing, clearly and logically.   _____

Youthful nature. I am capable of tackling work with enthusiasm and a high level of energy.   _____

Zest. I look forward to enjoying my business, the people I will be dealing with, and the resulting fruits of my labor.   _____

Although this is not a test, merely a tool to provide you with information about your entrepreneurial profile, there are immediate clues to your future as a business owner in the responses you have given.

If you have indicated fifteen or more strong traits, there is a good possibility that you have been involved in your own business in the past or, at least, have worked in a managerial capacity for someone else. You have the positive personality traits required to be a successful business owner. If you have between eight and fifteen "S" responses, you are basically a positive and directed person and should not have any problem with improving certain areas to increase your personal business success potential.

If you have fewer than eight "S" responses, this is an indication that finding a complementary business partner who can support your goals may be an option worth considering. ■

Notes

Key Points

_____

_____

_____

_____

Personal Thoughts

_____

_____

_____

_____

_____

_____

Additional Research

_____

_____

_____

_____

_____

3

Choosing the Right Business

Selecting the type of business to start is one of your primary steps in becoming an entrepreneur. It is not predicated on luck, although we've all heard about someone who just fell into a certain business opportunity and was able to make it a success. For the most part, however, it is a conscious decision based on personality, abilities and interests.

You want a business which suits your goals and personal lifestyle so it will be enjoyable. You must remember that you will be spending a lot of time and energy getting it off the ground, so it is important that you are doing something that you like.

Experience is not what happens to a person.
It is what a person does with
what has happened to them in the past.

Anonymous

Whether or not you have decided on the type of business you want to own and operate, it is advisable to prepare a Business Capabilites Application (BCA). Similar in nature to a job application, your personal Business Capabilities Application will give you a good idea of skills you have gained through education, jobs, and hobbies which can be of great importance in helping you find the right opportunity.

Your Application is a personal research tool, so it should be written out after serious consideration and analysis of the categories indicated below. Give yourself plenty of time to work on the BCA. Once you have written your answers, put them aside for a few days and then review them to see if there is anything crucial you might have left out the first time.

Education. Be sure to include specific courses which have had an impact on career decisions, as well as any courses that might prove useful in the running of your business (art, book-keeping, management training, etc.) Also, indicate seminars or workshops you have attended, which increased your knowledge of specialized areas of business.

Work experience. Outline the jobs you have held, what your exact responsibilities were and what you enjoyed most about each job. List any work habits and character traits which proved to be helpful in accomplishing your goals while holding these positions.

Health background. This is basically necessary only if you have a history of illness or any physical limitation which could affect your choice of a business. For example, if you have chronic back pain, you would not want to own a business that requires heavy lifting or being hunched over a work table for extended periods of time.

Hobbies. List hobbies you are currently pursuing and those you enjoyed in the past. Turning a hobby into a business is one of the most popular and successful ways of capitalizing on skills.

Volunteer experience. Include everything from political campaign support to chairing the PTA book drive. Volunteers typically delve into many areas which provide solid experience for running a business, such as telemarketing, working on a budget committee, organizing events or serving as a spokesperson. Outline your volunteer experiences carefully, indicating details of involvement.

Other interests. Use this category to make note of any additional skills and interests not included in the other categories. Those might include such areas as entertaining, a special ability with animals, children or seniors, your touch in the garden, a flair for flower arranging, etc.

If there is a faith that can move mountains,
it is faith in your own power.

Austrian author **Marie Ebner Von Eschenbach** wrote this phrase back in the mid-19th century and her words are as true today, especially for entrepreneurs.

Personal goals. Indicate the five most important areas—relating to your personal life—that you would like to accomplish over the next two years. These might include increased self-esteem, learning to complete projects, leaving a boring job, finding a new career, or having the opportunity to express a creative ability. Personal goals also include factors that cross over into business goals, such as earning enough money through self-employment to, say, purchase a new home within five years, or to gain experience in the business which enables you to write a book or develop a seminar program.

Business goals. Thinking in terms of owning your own business, write down at least five goals you would want to achieve, such as independence, financial security for retirement, national recognition, or recognizing a need and filling it.

Writing your skills, experiences, interests, and goals down on paper may provide just the spark needed to help you zero in on the perfect business. Once you have completed the Business Capabilities Application and reviewed it several days later, go back through and review the information with a colored marker in hand. Underline or circle any details that strike you as being particularly enjoyable.

You should see a pattern starting to emerge, such as an interest in working with people, or perhaps a preference for working outdoors. You are now half-way to finding a business suited to your personality and lifestyle. It has been proven that people who *enjoy* what they are doing are more successful than those who participate in a business simply because it seems like a good way to make money.

Looking at the Possibilities

The next step is to make a list of all the possible business opportunities that fit in with the information on your Business Capabilities Application. Here you must take into consideration how much time and energy you are willing to put into the business and what you expect in return over a short-term period, such as securing your position in the local business community, as well as over the long haul, e.g., a flexible schedule based on being in the economic position to hire employees.

Say, for example, you like to sleep until noon, enjoy preparing exciting new recipes for friends, have minimal start-up capital, but expect to see favorable financial rewards from your business. Your first idea for a business might be to open a restaurant.

However, owning a restaurant generally means getting started at 6 a.m. to prepare for lunch crowds. In addition, the expense of setting up an average family-style restaurant is conservatively estimated to be $50,000 ... and that is before you start hiring serving personnel and launching a major advertising campaign to let the local population know that you are now in business.

Taking these factors into account, it would appear that, because of your sleeping habits and low cash resources, restaurant ownership would be out of the question.

However, other possibilities to consider would be a catering company which could be run from your home, developing a specialized food product to manufacture and distribute which would give you the time flexibility you desire, or creating a unique dinner delivery service, where you prepare the meals and deliver them to working families, homebound seniors and other clientele you obtain through a carefully designed marketing program.

Narrowing the Choices

Once you have developed your list of possible businesses, the next step is to rate them in order of priority, according to your personal and business goals. Make a list of the possibilities running down the left side of a sheet of paper and note your goals across the top. Give each business a rating of one to ten as it relates to the goals, running horizontally across the page. Then add up the scores. The businesses with the highest scores are the ones you should explore further as having solid potential.

Check your listing of goals once more to ensure that you have included everything. If so, you can now start to research the strong contenders in your search for the business choice that best matches your needs and desires.

When conducting your research, ask friends and family members to provide their thoughts on which of the businesses they can see you operating successfully, and talk to the owners of similar businesses and ask them to share their experiences.

Ask for input from experts, such as your attorney, and representatives the Service Corps of Retired Executives (SCORE) through the nearest Small Business Administration office listed under U.S. Government in the front of your telephone book.

Finally, trust your intuition about the top contenders. Since you are the one who will be living with the business day-in and day-out, your final selection must be one that satisfies your goals, meets the criteria for growth potential, and features the kind of management and production tasks that you can easily handle. ■

Notes

Key Points

_____

_____

_____

Personal Thoughts

_____

_____

_____

_____

_____

Additional Research

_____

_____

_____

_____

4

Starting Your Telemarketing Service Bureau

An Overview of the Business

In its simplest definition, telemarketing is controlled use of the telephone to sell a product or service. This young, $100 billion a year business concept is generally used in conjunction with one or more additional sales tools, such as advertisements, catalogs, brochures, or letters. It's a business that you can easily get into and start realizing incredible profits in a very short period of time. Using the basic telemarketing techniques and

---

Overview of Telemarketing

This is a relatively young industry that is growing in leaps and bounds as large and small companies realize the benefits of using a telemarketing system for sales, customer service and long-term profits.

'Shoestring' Start-up Investment: (using home telephone)	$ 500
Average Start-up Investment: (small office/two shifts)	$ 15,000
High Start-up Investment: (computerized systems)	$ 50,000
Break-even Point:	Varies, but figure no more than 18 months
Average Annual Gross Revenues:	$ 25,000 to $80,000
Potential Annual Gross Revenues:	$150,000+

---

business information outlined in this book, you can be a part of this exciting, fast-growing industry.

More and more independent telemarketing services are cropping up across the country and helping business owners recognize how profitable it can be to have access to their clientele in the personal manner offered by the telephone. And rather than go to the trouble, time, and expense of setting up in-house telemarketing centers, these business executives are happy to share their profits with professional independent service owners.

Taking orders, handling consumer problems and inquiries, or test-marketing a new idea . . . all of these activities and more can be handled by a telemarketing service firm.

Whether your desire is to be a hands-on, self-employed business owner, or the absentee owner of an enterprise that employs five or more telemarketing representatives, this may be your key to success and independence.

Sales Tip to Keep in Mind

The very worst thing a prospective customer can say is "no." You can convince them through shrewd selling techniques to change that to a "yes!"

The telemarketing service business is unique because it can be so many different things. For one, it is a service many types of business need, although they may not be aware of the benefits since the industry is still so young . . . until you educate them. Therefore, starting a telemarketing service is a great way to capitalize on both the personal and business contacts you may already have in your area.

At this point, there is no end in sight to the expansion of telemarketing, a business that has as many options, outlined below, as there are telephone systems available. It is a business with tremendous growth potential and one that you can get started on right now.

Getting Started

Surprisingly, it is also quite simple to get going—requiring no special education or degrees, and very little in the way of equipment, if you want to start on a "shoestring" basis. If this type of business sounds interesting to you, you've already made a good first step by studying this book and the suggestions, news of technological breakthroughs and options detailed within.

We will also give you start-up ideas based on your available capital and offer suggestions that can help you get started no matter what your financial situation may be.

Actually, there are no other special qualifications required that can keep you from this exciting and fun new venture. Maybe you like the idea of a business you could actually get started and run from your own home during the early days? Maybe you've always been told that your telephone manner and voice is exceptional?

Perhaps you have a background or interest in communications or sales and enjoy talking with people? Or possibly you recognize the incredible future in telemarketing. Whatever the reason, this is a business that is fun and profitable.

What Exactly is Telemarketing?

We asked a random sampling of the population what telemarketing means to them. The majority of the 100 people surveyed say they visualize a roomful of people systematically working their way through telephone books of various cities and towns, calling unsuspecting recipients for donations or trying to sell newspaper subscriptions.

Direct selling or solicitation is certainly one aspect of the business, but it by no means should be viewed in a negative way nor is it as limited as many seem to think. Over the past few years, telemarketing has become a highly respected business that can involve a broad spectrum of effective programs and techniques for small and large businesses, including the following:

1. *Setting appointments for a sales staff,* especially in the insurance industry, for real estate and home improvements. Names of prospective clients are usually generated by a promotional letter with a mail-back card indicating interest, from entry forms in contests, registrants names collected for an open house "door prize", or specific lists of names rented from a professional list broker.

2. *Generating brand new leads* by making "cold calls" to names and numbers selected at random from telephone books. This involves educating the potential client and getting assurance that they can be contacted in the future for special promotions or further information.

3. *Conducting general market research* to find out what people eat, drink, enjoy on television, or hundreds of other lifestyle particulars that can be used to develop promotional campaigns and other sales material for your specific purposes.

4. *Handling collections of overdue accounts.* Using the telephone makes it personal and is generally more effective in dealing with slow-paying customers than communicating through the mail.

5. *Verifying orders.* Calling a customer to confirm their order and give them an expected delivery date or work date pro-

vides an opportunity to sell additional services or products since they have purchased once, and can now be considered a captive audience.

6. *Maintaining customer relations* by calling to see if people are satisfied with what you sold them previously. Another excellent opportunity to introduce them to something new or updated.

7. *Handling certain public relations tasks,* such as announcing a major change in name, address, or product line of a company. Telemarketing has also been used effectively in announcing mergers, or sales to stockholders and clients of large companies.

A Look at Inbound Telemarketing

Most of the above-mentioned activities are considered outgoing telemarketing, where an operator or representative calls the client or prospective customer.

There are, in addition, a number of incoming telemarketing activities which can mean impressive long-range profits and other benefits for a company. Most of these are dependent on a toll-free 800 number and include:

1. *Basic order-taking.* It has been proven time and time again that the availability of an 800 number in an ad or a catalog will increase sales and/or response by fourty to sixty percent over mail-only returns. And, as indicated above, dealing with orders over the telephone can lead to additional sales.

2. *Customer service.* This involves handling service problems, hearing complaints and positive input which can be used in refining products and fine-tuning marketing programs, as well as providing general information to inquiries from the public.

3. *Building leads from inquiries* and, even better, being able to qualify them as solid potential customers during that initial call with a simple series of questions designed for the product.
4. *Taking reservations,* selling subscriptions and accepting pledges or donations.
5. *Updating customer lists.* By providing an easily accessed 800 number, customers will generally feel no qualms about calling with a change of address and name or other pertinent information.
6. *Gauging the effectiveness of advertising* or public relations by offering something free—a booklet, coupon or similar enticement—to people who call.

Telemarketing is More Than Just Sales

Obviously, all of the aspects of both incoming and outgoing telemarketing require qualified, positive telephone representatives to insure that the effort satisfies bottom-line goals. A program is only as effective as the people managing and implementing it; we cover these important areas in greater detail later in this guide.

What You Need to Get Started

- Telephone System
- Prospective Buyer Leads
- A Product or Service
- A Script
- Phone Skills
- Control Documents

If you have ever been involved with sales, you know that most of us use the telephone in one way or another to sell. However, in the majority of cases it could be considered a casual or soft approach, such as regular "checking in" with potential or established clients to keep yourself in their consciousness or even to setting up an appointment to see them. Usually, however, the call is not the primary sales focus; that comes when you are face-to-face with your customer.

Telemarketing, on the other hand, is specific. It uses scripts developed especially for the product or service being pro-

---

If your goal is long-term involvement in the business, the time to begin developing success-oriented habits is from the very beginning. With that in mind, here's one checklist:

1. Work with products and services which appeal to consumer's needs to give you the edge on sales.
2. Have your clients prepare creative promotional material that provides clear and simple details about the product(s) or service(s) being sold.
3. Develop an order system which is convenient and easy to use.
4. Ensure that "Customer Service" is the phrase of the day .... every day.

---

moted and depends, in fact, on the telephone as the actual sales medium. The representative is just a voice on the other end of the phone and must be able to make themselves understood in a convincing and honest way in a very short period of time.

Whereas first impressions in most sales situations are made through wardrobe, body language and other visuals, telephone representatives do not have these luxuries ... it's all based on the aural (hearing) "image" made in the first few seconds.

Difficult? Not really. In fact, many salespeople claim they prefer working on the telephone because they can get to the main issue much faster than in more socially oriented field calls. But, telemarketing not only saves time, it saves energy (no driving, no parking problems, no walking from location to location) and, even better, saves money that would have been spent on expenses.

Gardens were not made by singing
"Oh, how beautiful"
and sitting in the shade.

Rudyard Kipling

Why Telemarketing Works

In fact, money is basically how the whole thing started. The OPEC oil embargo of 1973 resulted in an alarming increase in energy costs, which forced up the cost of sales, since most involved travel.

By the early 1980s, the cost of a personal sales call to a business client was more than $100, including gas, food, incidentals and related administrative expenses. By the mid-1980s, the cost of that same sales call was over $200 and rising.

Telephone rates were not increasing in the same dramatic way as energy. A telephone sales call in 1985 averaged less than $8 and savvy business managers soon recognized the potential of this under-utilized medium.

So, using the telephone as a sales tool not only generated higher volume while lowering the cost per sale, it opened up a broader market than had ever been available before ... almost everyone could be reached by telephone, thereby creating an unlimited market.

In addition, since those early days it has served as the basis for an exciting new business that has nowhere to go but up! In the past decade, telemarketing has grown into a $100 billion+ industry (based on annual sales generated) that is destined to continue growing in the coming years.

A Few Proven
Telemarketing Successes

Advertising Sales	Pest Control
Automobile Parts	Real Estate
Books	Some Food Products
House Cleaning Services	Solar Heating Systems
Insurance	Stocks & Bonds
Jewelry	Office Supplies
Magazine Subscriptions	Office Equipment
Makeup	Wines
Records	Toys

In fact, a recent article in *Business Week* magazine estimated that more than eight million new jobs will be available in telemarketing by the beginning of the 21st century.

When it first starting enjoying popularity as a sales tool, telemarketing was generally established as a single department set up within the confines of a large corporation. This is still the case today ... most major companies that deal with the public have in-house telemarketing systems and staffs set up to deal exclusively with their customers.

However, a new opportunity exists for savvy entrepreneurs who want to get wired into this fascinating business; owning an independent professional telemarketing service that operates on a contract basis. The market is certainly out there—from mom-and-pop businesses that need only periodic service to test their market or promote a new product, all the way up to large corporations that have an ongoing need, but do not want the expense and responsibility of an internal arrangement.

In several cases, we ran across owner/operators of telephone answering services who had incorporated an independent telemarketing service as an adjunct to their business. We spoke with several people who function out of their homes strictly as freelance telemarketers; generally hiring part-time employees to help them when they get a long-term account. We ran across a few who function as contractors; setting up one-person service bureaus for major companies which pay them a fee in addition to reimbursing them for expenses.

Still others could be considered mavericks, starting "bullpen" operations with rows of telephone-laden desks to accommodate three to four shifts of telemarketers selling everything from cookbooks and calculators to vacation homes and investments. And the owners of these operations are making money hand over fist based on a flat service rate *plus* a percentage of every sale!

What It Takes to Succeed in the Business

What kind of qualifications do you need to get into telemarketing? Well, there are no professional or academic requirements of any kind, though having a Ph.D. in Common Sense won't hurt you any. And while there is no profile that can determine whether you're a good candidate for a telemarketing operation, if you possess certain business traits you'll most likely do just fine. These traits include:

- A genuine enjoyment of spending hours on the telephone. It also helps if you consider yourself a "people" person who is as willing to listen to prospective customers as to convince them to sign up, send in a check or give you their credit card number.
- A basic understanding of telephone sales techniques, as outlined in this book.
- Organizational ability.
- Motivation and perseverance, because as with any business, success doesn't happen overnight (although the right client and/or product can result in fast profits).
- Willingness to work hard and often for long hours, especially when one (or more) of your telemarketing crew members fails to show up for a shift, which typically happens in the middle of an important campaign.
- Flexibility and the ability to handle a variety of tasks, such as selling the concept of telemarketing to company executives, hiring and training phone representatives, and maintaining comprehensive records of hour-to-hour and day-to-day activities.
- Awareness of the client's needs, as well as the ability to zero in on what prospective customers (those on the other end of the telephone lines) want.

Although an extensive background in marketing is not a requirement, it certainly wouldn't hurt you to take a class at your local community college or adult education center just to get an idea of what marketing can do. While most of the telemarketing service owners we spoke with had any formal training (a few had worked as telemarketing reps for major companies), they claimed that understanding the marketing process—through reading or a college class—gave them an edge when selling their services to potential clients.

As previously mentioned, the time to begin developing success-oriented habits is from day one. Organization, motiva-

tion and perseverance are as important when you are researching the feasibility of your new business as when you are up and
running.

Profit Potential

How much money you make in telemarketing depends, again,
on the clients you round up and the amount of time you spend
selling their product or service. If you work only a few hours a
week out of your home, you might augment your monthly
income by a couple of hundred dollars. (A home-based business will offer more profit potential in the beginning because of
low fixed costs—the rent and utilities, for example, are taken
care of— but we'll get to that later on.)

On the other hand, some of the most successful one-person
operations that have outgrown living rooms earn as much as
$50,000 to $70,000 and more a year. One of the newest telemarketing service companies in the country maintains a low
profile in downtown Wichita. This "bullpen" is bringing in
gross revenues of $250,000 per month for its three clients after
only six months in business. It isn't difficult to see what a $1,500
per month retainer and fifteen percent of all sales is going to do
for this five-person operation over the next year!

Looking at the Profit Picture

Here is a scenerio of an operation where two well-trained
telephone representatives are each on the phones seven hours
a day making outgoing calls to sell a product. The reps make
an average of 15 calls each an hour, so let's see what can be done
in a week.

7 hours a day x 2 reps	=	14 selling hours per day
14 hours a day x 5 week days	=	70 selling hours per week
70 hours x 15 calls per hour	=	1050 calls per week

If the reps are selling one out of every three calls (350) at an average sale of $29.95, the service will be grossing $10,482.50 per week for the client. Based on a weekly service retainer of $300, and fifteen percent of the gross revenues, the service is billing $1,872 per week, or about $7,500 a month for the one account, if the sales momentum is maintained. (Other billing options and ideas are outlined in Chapter 16, Pricing for Profits, for your consideration.)

Of course, overhead expenses for the week must be deducted from the income. In this scenario, let us assume the following (please be aware that, in most cases, income and expense would be broken down on a monthly basis):

Base salary for reps at $4 per hour	
$4 x 70 hours	$ 280.00
Commission to reps; $2 per sale	
350 sales x $2	700.00
Rent (one week)	150.00
Telephone expense	200.00
Office expenses	25.00
Advertising expense	50.00
Taxes, etc.	25.00
Total	$1,430.00

Even after deducting overhead expenses (excluding owner's draw), there is a net profit of $442! Not bad for one account. Now, imagine the potential with three, four or six accounts. Although it would be necessary to hire and pay additional phone reps, all of your other operating costs, except for the telephone charges, would basically be covered, increasing your profit margin.

Something to consider as you formulate your start-up plan is how you want your business to grow; quickly yet deliberately, slow and steady, or as you happen to get accounts.

Obviously the third option is too hit-and-miss to spell success in the long run, however, both the first two options are feasible, depending on personal preference, expansion capital, and long-term goals.

Ask yourself these important questions: If your profit is directly proportional to your sales volume, how much must you let your sales expand to realize maximum profit potential? Do you have the wherewithal to support the growth you envision? Will the market support the direction in which you want to grow?

While you ponder the preceding points, consider this: Most businesses experience peaks and valleys relative to the ups and downs of their respective industries. Here the news is bright ... telemarketing offers you excellent long-term growth potential because the industry itself can only get bigger.

Telephone Sales Tip to Keep in Mind

*When you are "working the phones,"
always have a glass of water nearby
to prevent dry mouth and a parched throat
that may affect your speaking voice.*

The Comfort Factor

It's obvious that the American public is getting more comfortable about buying over the telephone, because sales generated through telemarketing efforts have been increasing steadily over the past few years ... just take a few minutes to watch the phenomenal success of Home Shopping shows on the cable networks. They are bringing in millions of dollars a year—all via the telephone!

The Census Bureau estimates that the U.S. population will rise to 300 million people by the year 2000. That means about 87 million more folks than there are today, and all of them will want or need something that can be sold by telephone. In fact, more and more of them won't want to take care of business—from banking to buying—any other way, according to predictions.

The trend is on the upswing—already buying by telephone has become a reality for many people who either can't get out to shop or simply do not want to hassle the traffic and the crowds.

As we see it, there's no better time to start exploring the potential of that market than today. Be ready for the 21st century by promoting your services as an independent telemarketer to small and large businesses with a need to get in touch with the American buying population. Turn your telephone into a gold line! ■

Notes

Key Points

_____

_____

_____

Personal Thoughts

_____

_____

_____

_____

_____

Additional Research

_____

_____

_____

_____

_____

5

A Marketing Overview

Now that you have selected the kind of business you want to own, it is important to explore the need for it. A process called *marketing research* will provide you with the information you need to develop your telemarketing service, plan methods of promotion, and set prices which are tailored to the audience you hope to attract.

In addition, your marketing research will provide you with information that will help when you are making decisions about a location, hours of operation, the specific types of services to promote, and how to gear your advertising.

Identifying Your Market

The process of identifying your audience may seem to be an extremely complex process, however, you can develop a perfectly workable and valuable marketing report using the guidelines which follow and adapting them to your particular situation. Basically, there are five factors used to target the market:

Population. The number of households or businesses in the region you are considering as a target for your business is crucial as you must have a sufficient population base to produce the sales you need to generate a profit. Equally important is the circulation and age range of readers of any magazine where you will be focusing your advertising on for specific products. If, for example, you are planning to sell products for infants, a publication whose readership is largely of retirement age would be unappropriate. It would, however, work in your favor if you are promoting health products or even gift items.

Income. Your potential customers must have the income to purchase goods and services. Consumers in the 35-65 age group generally have considerable income which they spend on household items, personal grooming and sporting goods. This is not to discount the over-65 age group, a good-sized and growing segment of the nation's population which, depending on the region, has discretionary income (money to spend after taxes and necessities), or the 18-35 age group, which is a desireable market for clothing, personal and recreational items.

Competition. The recent heavy promotion of "Tennis Bracelets" popularized by Chris Evert-Lloyd made it difficult for late-comers to make a dent in the market. This is almost always the case and, therefore, competition shouldn't be a negative factor. Rather, it should spur you on to stretch your creativity by coming up with something brand new or a similar product or service that is superior to those being offered by the competition—either through quality, selection, or price.

Product or service market match. Basically, this means that you must be able to attract those consumers whom you have the resources to serve. As an example, if your idea of the perfect business involves national distribution of your patented weight-training equipment, you must:

1. Reach an audience that is receptive and interested in body building through a carefully designed advertising campaign, and
2. Have the financing available to supply and ship the product.

Desire. Your objective is to match your product or service to the needs and desires of a particular group of consumers who will be responsive.

It is often difficult to figure out exactly what your target market wants. However, through observation of what the competition is doing, it should be possible to recognize a need.

Market Research Techniques

Large corporations often have in-house marketing staffs which conduct extensive research on a continuing basis to ensure that the products or services being offered are in line with the marketplace.

Obviously, this is an expensive and time-consuming process; one that you undoubtedly want to avoid.

Through several easy and inexpensive methods, you can find out everything you want to know about your potential market. The first step, however, is to determine exactly what information you need. It might be trends in population figures or regional economy or how many people are active in a particular hobby.

The nearest Census Bureau office and your local Chamber of Commerce are consistently good sources for regional statistics. The reference librarian at the public library can steer you towards other local data and fact sheets which will give you the specifics you seek. In addition, the Small Business Administration compiles extensive marketing information, in addition to material on operating procedures for specific types of businesses.

Check the Directory of Trade Associations at the library to find the name and address of associations for the telemarketing industry (or check the Resources listed at the end of this book). These trade boards exist to provide associates with marketing statistics, management tips and a wealth of valuable information. Often it only takes a phone call to get more details than you could ever use.

Another excellent source of information on population, income, and sales figures is the annual survey of buying power published by *Sales and Marketing Management* magazine, which breaks the information down by county and cities in the United States.

Other Resources

The advertising departments of magazines and newspapers undoubtedly have Media Kits available for potential advertisers, which they will gladly send you upon request. These packets contain a breakdown of their advertising rates and specifications, a description of why advertising with them is to your benefit and, most important, a profile of their readership. A friendly conversation with one of their salespeople should give you a wealth of data.

Talking with the people from whom you will be buying supplies, equipment and products is another excellent source. They can give you a good run-down on trends, as well as an overview of current sales figures for their products. Since they are hoping you will eventually use them as a supplier for your business, they will be more than happy to give you free information.

Five Factors Used to Target your Market

1. Population
2. Income
3. Competition
4. Market Match
5. Desire

It is, of course, often possible to gauge what the competition is doing and to wean information from them. There are two approaches when talking to people who are soon to be in direct competition. The best one is to be up-front and honest about your business plans and appeal to their sense of "industy spirit."

Surprisingly, you will find the direct approach works in the majority of cases as most people are genuinely interested in and supportive of others trying to make it in their field. It is better for everyone if "industry" standards are maintained and competitors have a healthy rapport. And, except in extreme situations such as a very small community, there is generally enough business to go around. It shouldn't be difficult to capture your share of the market, especially if you can develop something unique to attract it.

On the other hand, if competitors are less than receptive, it may be necessary to partake in a bit of super-sleuthing to get the information you want. A little brainstorming with friends should result in a few good ideas if you find it necessary to resort to investigative techniques.

The "Focus" Group

If you really want to go into depth with your marketing study, you might consider gathering together a group of people (family members, a social or business group, or friends) for a "focus" session to determine whether your product or service will match the needs of the prospective audience. This involves presenting your proposed business idea, with service examples if available, and creating a questionnaire that calls for specific answers from the group members.

This method is often used by major companies when they are testing new products or services and, in fact, there are private companies around the nation who do nothing but put focus groups together and set up testing sites in stores, shopping malls, and on street corners to obtain spontaneous and objective input from potential consumers.

The questions you would want to include on your questionnaire would ideally cover such aspects as how often members of the focus group have used a similar service or product in the past, what they liked about it, what they found to be unsatisfactory, how they feel it could have been improved, whether they would be willing to try another, their age, income, and any specifics that relate to your proposed business.

With the telemarketing aspect, the questions might include a breakdown of the top three reasons people in your focus group would consider using a telemarketing service (order-taking, customer service, research and surveys), how they would expect to be treated by telemarketing representatives as a prospective customer, and how they go about finding telemarketing service bureaus to consider using (Yellow Pages, referrals, newspaper ads). This kind of information will give you an immediate edge on the competition when you are ready to start advertising.

Analyzing your Marketing Research

The bottom line in conducting your research is that you want to zero in on information which provides insights on the potential for your business idea before you invest time, money, and energy in setting it up.

If, for example, you were considering focusing your telemarketing agency services on contracting out as a customer relations inbound line for major oil companies, and your research indicated that ninety percent of the oil companies prefer hearing from their customers through the mail, you would definitely want to reconsider the validity of your concept. On the other hand, if your marketing research pointed out that sixty percent of the oil companies recognize the need for telecommunications via a toll-free 800 number, the potential for your service would obviously be much greater. Promoting it would ensure a profitable venture.

Buy an inexpensive notebook to help you keep track of your marketing data. Use a separate page for each category you are researching. The notebook will serve as your personal, on-going market study to be reviewed and amended as your business grows and the audience you are serving changes.

The greatest thing in the world is not so much where we stand as in what direction we are moving.

Oliver Wendell Holmes

Plan to update information pages as new studies are published (generally an annual event) indicating changes in population, economy, or buying and spending trends. Most newspapers publish synopses of local, state and federal studies of this nature, so maintaining your notebook shouldn't be a problem. You should also reserve several pages to record comments and suggestions from clients once your business is established, which will help you personalize your business to the market and keep you a step ahead of the competition.

Spend as much time as needed to feel comfortable about your marketing project. For some people, this might mean two hours at the City Clerk's office, while others may want to devote a week or more to gathering details and analyzing it to incorporate into their business plan.

The important point is that the results of your research are comprehensive enough to provide you with concrete information on who your potential customers are and how you can best reach them. ■

6

Potential Telemarketing Clients

The telephone technology revolution is in full swing and can be expected to grow dramatically over the next decade. Today, in fact, the telephone is considered to be the fastest growing marketing and sales resource at our disposal. Not only is it a powerful technological tool—especially when used in conjunction with a computer—it still maintains its personal quality and the intimacy inherent in the two-way conversation.

The increased demand for telemarketing services is primarily based on the incredible response that is attainable by a highly motivated crew of telephone salespeople. Whether used as a sole sales or marketing tool, or used in conjunction with direct mail or other promotional campaigns, telemarketing is both cost efficient and time effective.

There is a growing awareness in the nation of the importance of telemarketing. More and more business owners and executives realize that having a competent crew of telemarketing representatives supporting and promoting products and services over the telephone gives them the opportunity to develop a personal relationship with hundreds of thousands of past, present, and future clients.

As the owner of a telemarketing service bureau, you will want to know who your potential customers are and how you can best reach them. In addressing this question, take a moment to think about friends, relatives and neighbors who own their own businesses.

Has anyone you know recently become an insurance agent, real estate broker, or become involved in a political campaign? All of these people conceivably have the need for telemarketing services—they simply may not be aware of it until you inform them of the benefits.

Make a list of everyone you know. Even if the names on your list seem unrealistic as far as potential clients go, keep in mind that they may know someone else who would be interested in using your telemarketing services. Your list will serve you both in pre-planning your business approach and in ongoing client recruiting.

Your list should include the names of the following people. Undoubtedly you will think of other contacts which are not outlined below, but this will give you a strong starting point.

- Immediate family members
- Relatives who live in the area
- Friends
- Aquaintances from work, school, church or social groups
- Retailers who may be having collection problems
- Acquaintances through sports or hobbies
- Your doctor, dentist, plumber and local service organizations

Talk to everyone on your list to find out whether they have a need for, or even truly understand the incredible impact of telemarketing, or if they can give you the name of someone they know who might be a potential client. Give out business cards and brochures and ask everyone to pass them along—people love to help and will probably be happy to lend a hand in getting your business off the ground.

In recruiting business for your telemarketing service bureau, you can be extremely effective by taking advantage of your own expertise. Conducting a concentrated promotional and marketing campaign by telephone for 20 working days should bring you a guaranteed clientele. Actually, in this case, the call-direct mail-call method will be the most effective way to reach the decision-makers of the companies you are interested in servicing.

Serious Effort Will Pay Off

Start by making 15 to 25 calls every day as determined from your "Potential Client" list, as outlined on the previous page. Make this your primary goal for each of the 20 days of the campaign (add extra days according to response, goals and your workload). Use the local telephone book to find the phone numbers of, for example, every small business or major corporation within a 50-mile radius you feel would benefit from incorporating telemarketing into their management programs.

You might compile the list yourself, from Dun & Bradstreet lists of top firms in their industries or, perhaps, based on a specific list you have rented from a list broker (more on direct mail in Chapter 22, Advertising Your Business). If you are like most people, however, your list will be a composite of several resources and the result of a lot of effort.

Call and find out exactly who the decision-maker is with each company—the receptionist should be able to give you the names of important parties and their respective titles within the chain of command. Once you get past the receptionist and the secretaries or administrative assistants, explain to the decision-maker that you will be sending out a letter (or brochure or packet of information) *today*.

Tell them you will call back next week to answer any questions and set up an appointment. Be sure to cover all the basics and take care of any initial telemarketing inquiries during this first call.

Mail out the material immediately. Mark the envelope personal and confidential to improve its chances of getting through to the recipient. Call back the following week as promised to ensure that the information was received and read. At that point, ask if there are any questions. If so, answer them.

If not, review the benefits of using your service bureau, offer a first-time discount, one month's free set-up charges or a similar incentive, and then try to schedule an appointment to explain your telemarketing service in more detail.

If you don't get an appointment with the first call, offer to keep in touch, suggesting that you will call back in six months to see if the circumstances have changed. If you are feeling especially confident and the party on the other end is friendly, ask if they know of any other business owners or company executives who might be interested in talking with you.

The Phone Is a Way of Life

Overall, you should find the majority of people to be interested in learning more about telemarketing, at least. Americans have become more receptive over the past few years to the idea of conducting business over the telephone, including shopping, voting, learning, and communications at all levels. There are very few people who don't have at least one telephone at home and another at their office.

And nobody can resist the ringing of a telephone . . . everyone has a desire to find out who is calling. The benefit for telemarketers is that the telephone gives them carte blanche into millions of homes and offices, they don't have to travel for hours and possibly find that they have been stood up, and nobody has to get dressed up for the meeting. In fact, we spoke with one home-based telemarketer who claims he does his best work right after jogging—before his shower and still wearing his jogging clothes—while his mind is fresh, energized and clear. Although it isn't recommended that you and your tele-marketing representatives show up for work in exactly this condition, it goes to show that this is a business that does not stand on usual corporate dress ceremony!

Another demographic aspect in your favor as a tele-marketer is that the "baby boom" generation has come of age.

This group has come to accept the telephone as a way of life and is receptive to the whole concept of telemarketing.

There are endless possibilities in the business world, which will account for ninety-five percent of your business, if properly cultivated. Once you have handled a few practice-run telemarketing campaigns for friends or relatives who are involved in business, politics, or charities, you will be ready to approach commercial accounts, such as:

- Owners of new businesses who may not have considered the benefit of using telemarketing to announce their store or service and, later, to keep their name in the public consciousness.
- Charitable organizations, which are dependent on top-flight fundraising tactics to attract big-ticket contributors to take care of operating capital as well as the actual financing of the charity.
- Real estate offices that are constantly trying to find more houses to sell through neighborhood telemarketing campaigns.
- Insurance offices that need appointments set for their agents.
- Doctors, dentists, and other professionals who want to build their business or who have become frustrated with trying to collect past due billing via the mail.
- Political rallies and volunteer events, such as selling tickets to the annual firemen's rodeo in your town.
- Social Clubs and Networking Groups, such as the Chamber of Commerce, which constantly recruit new members.
- Major corporations that will utilize telemarketing for everything from order-taking, sales, and customer service, to the handling of marketing surveys and follow-up with past customers to reinforce name recognition and stay ahead of the competition.

As you become more involved with setting up your tele-marketing service, you will begin to see possibilities everywhere. The best thing is to start making notes and to add to them regularly, no matter how obscure an idea may seem, so you have a ready-made mailing list by the time you are ready to seriously promote the service. ■

Notes

Target audience

_____

_____

_____

_____

Publications for advertising

_____

_____

_____

_____

_____

_____

Additional research information

_____

_____

_____

_____

_____

Review

- I have completed my entrepreneurial profile to determine my strengths and weaknesses. _____

- My friends and/or relatives have given me additional input based on the profile. _____

- I am aware of the advantages and disadvantages of going into business for myself. _____

- I have prepared and reviewed my Business Capabilities Application. _____

- Time is not a problem; I can easily devote the time I'll need to build my business. _____

- The important people in my life are supportive of my decision. _____

- I have analyzed my personal cash flow to insure that I can support myself and my family for at least six months, or until the business is solvent. _____

- I feel confident about my future as a business owner at this point. _____

- I know what people want as far as my business is concerned. _____

- I have conducted informal studies to determine my potential customers and their needs. _____

- I have analyzed the competition, know what they offer, and have a general idea about their success ratio. _____

- I have done my marketing research and know how to get in touch with the audience I want to reach. _____

- I have contacted the trade association for my industry and have accumulated facts and figures regarding the pros and cons of starting my own business. _____

- I feel confident that my product or service is salable. _____

7

Location: Commercial vs. Home-Based

One of the best things about the telemarketing service business is that you don't need a fancy location or prominently placed (and therefore expensive) storefront associated with most retail operations. All you need is space for the number of stations your client base can support; and this can be operated out of almost any well organized space—even from your own home!

The amount of space you will need depends largely on number of clients you are serving and, conversely, the number of telemarketing representatives you must hire, as well as the type of equipment you buy or lease. There are, however, several other factors to consider, as well.

Because much of your success will depend on accurate and up-to-date record-keeping (incoming and outgoing calls, number of sales, names and addresses of customers, etc.), efficiency in your work space is also important to consider. The flow of paperwork from sales call to client must be well organized.

Each work station will require a telephone system, room for presentation materials, such as product information book, sales and survey or order forms, and possibly a computer monitor and keyboard.

It is suggested that you allocate a minimum of 100 square feet for every four working representatives, although most planning experts claim that each rep should have at least 50 square feet to accommodate a desk, chair, bulletin board, file cabinet, and other sales tools.

In addition, you must be sure that there is enough room separating representatives so they are not disturbed or interrupted by each other's conversations.

Outside your home, the cost for work space varies. To locate in a highrise office building in the business center of town, expect to pay as much $8 a square foot.

However, as mentioned above, nothing elaborate is required to establish your telemarketing business and often work spaces can be found in out of the way places, even warehouse or loft situations. Prices for these tend to be much lower, usually around $2 per square foot per month and sometimes even less depending on the city and area of town.

No matter where you locate your telemarketing service bureau, sufficient and safe parking facilities should be a major consideration. Unlike other businesses, yours is one that will have employees coming and going at odd hours—from early in the morning to late at night. Providing a safe location for these employees is your responsibility and the lure of an inexpensive site must be offset by common sense about the nature of the business. Better safe than sorry.

Telephone Sales
Tips to Remember

- Secretaries can be your best friends or your worst enemies in this business. By treating them with the respect they deserve, you will find it easier to reach the decision-makers in companies.
- Many top sales reps claim that they "visualize" closing the sale—seeing themselves fill in the order form. This gives them the confidence to "assume the sale." Rather than asking, "Should I write that up?" they say, "I am writing that up as we speak!"
- Stay motivated by making a commitment to your daily call plan and try not to deviate no matter what comes up! Discipline is the key to success!

Inexpensive Ways to Start

You might also consider exploring the options listed below as a way to start. Later, when your business grows, you can establish your service bureau in a commercial location.

1. Restrict your business, at first, to only those jobs that permit you to do the majority of calling at the client's location, thereby saving money on telephone equipment and installation costs.
2. Hire out as a telemarketing consultant; going in and setting up a telemarketing center for companies with an ongoing need. This would involve helping them select the proper systems for the job, working with the long distance carrier to ensure top-quality service and hiring and training a telemarketing crew. This is a low overhead, minimal startup capital way of getting your business off the ground and establishing a reputation.
3. Scout the area where you live for businesses that have telephone systems set up, but also have empty offices for one reason or another, i.e., an insurance company that has many branch offices and, consequently, moves agents around from site to site.

It may be possible to rent a small space during prearranged time periods for your business or even to trade your telemarketing services in exchange for telephone usage. Since many of your calling hours are in the evening—after people have finished their 9:00 to 5:00 assignments, it may be possible to sublease a space from, say, 5:30 to 9:00 pm.

Before moving into a space or signing a sublease, make sure that electrical lines are adequate to handle high volume phoning, and that you have restrooms and convenient parking for any employees.

Also check with the landlord, even in a sublet situation, to be certain you can make improvements, e.g., built-in cubicles or storage cabinets, at your discretion as the business warrants it.

A Pleasant Background Makes a Difference

To increase productivity in the office, paint the walls a light color and provide good ventilation. A little background music, telemarketing service owners tell us, also helps to keep motivation high during slack periods and between sales calls, while reps are taking care of paperwork.

Despite the fact that there are hundreds of hot, smoky, windowless telemarketing "bullpens" or "boiler rooms" in existence, there is proof that the more comfortable and pleasant the environment, the greater the productivity of your reps.

Think about it; would you personally be more likely to do your best job in an crowded, airless room with green walls, shabby furniture, and second-rate telephone equipment, or in a cheerful, bright room with pictures on the wall, comfortable chairs, and access to a coffee pot?

You can increase your odds of being successful, as a sole owner, and once you start hiring reps to help you handle the workload, if you consider the following positive aspects when selecting a location:

- A room or suite of offices with windows, or at the very least, light colored walls and live greenery to bring the outdoors in.
- Heating for cool days and air conditioning or ventilation system for hot summer afternoons and to eliminate cigarette smoke.
- Individual work areas or cubicles for each rep; a place where they know they belong and can set up a picture of the kids or the dog.

- Secretarial or office chairs with adjustable height and back.
- Acoustic ceiling tiles, carpeting, and wall paneling will help dampen extraneous sound that might distract a rep during a sales call.
- A small refrigerator, coffee maker, and water cooler.
- Soft yet bright lighting that will reduce eyestrain and the possibility of headaches.
- Top-quality telephone systems that make the work as easy as possible.

These environmental necessities will, of course, cost you a little bit of money, but the long-term returns will quickly make you realize the importance of setting up a location that encourages productivity.

When a Client Wants to Stop By

It is possible that, now and then, one of your clients will be interested in visiting your operation. (According to service bureau owners we spoke with, however, this is a small percentage which becomes even smaller once your reputation is established. In most cases, you will secure an account by making the presentation of your services at *their* office.)

However, if they do suggest a tour of your premises, try not to be surprised; they may feel the need to ensure they are paying for professional telemarketing service. This is especially true if they are trying telemarketing for the first time.

So, whether you work out of your home or a commercial location, the most important thing to be able to display is a neat, comfortable environment that shows prospective clients that they will be paying for action and results . . . not expensive desks and computers or costly high-tech cubicle dividers. A strong sense of enthusiasm among your reps indicates high morale and high morale is indicative of sales, which is the main interest of every one of your clients.

Before You Sign a Lease

In all but the most unusual cases, such as renting your location from a family member or accepting a temporary agreement in a building that is for sale, you will be required to sign a lease before moving into your new location. The most desirable agreement for you as a new business owner is a one- to two-year lease with a renewal option at a guaranteed rate for rent increases over a five- to ten-year period.

Rent for a commercial location is established either on a flat rate or a percentage basis. Under the flat rate, rent is generally based on the square footage of the shop and on the location or, in some cases, on potential volume. The percentage base involves a base amount of rent plus a prearranged percentage of monthly sales.

Your lease will also cover a number of other points, such as the liabilities and responsibilities of the landlord and of you, the tenant; i.e., who is to pay for specific repairs, renovations, tax increases and utilities, etc.

The lease may contain stipulations about the hours of operation, insurance coverage, and assignation of the lease to another party (a sublet).

Before signing a lease to set up your business, make sure that gas, electrical and water lines are adequate enough to handle high volume usage, that you have restrooms and changing areas for employees, and convenient parking and loading areas.

Also check with the leasing agent to be certain you can make leasehold improvements, e.g., storage shelves, at your discretion as the business warrants it. It is recommended that you have an attorney review the lease carefully before you sign it. This will ensure that you understand all of the clauses, and to serve as a negotiator, if necessary.

Setting Up Your Business at Home

Short of disrupting family patterns on days when you are in the midst of a hot-and-heavy telemarketing campaign, there is a lot of appeal in operating your service out of your own home.

Thousands of successful businesses have been started in a basement, a spare room or on the kitchen table. Henry Ford, for example, founded the Ford Motor Company in his garage and Jean Nidetch started Weight Watchers in her living room as a support group for friends who wanted to lose extra pounds. Both of these businesses, and many more like them, became successful full-fledged corporations, despite humble beginnings.

The Advantages of Establishing a Home-Based Business

- Ability to start your business immediately
- Minimal start-up capital needed
- No rent or excessive set-up charges for utilities required
- Comfortable working conditions
- Reduced wardrobe expenses
- No commuting
- Tax benefits
- Elimination of office politics
- Flexibility and independence
- Full utilization and recognition of skills
- Low risk for trial and error

The Small Business Administration estimates that there are close to 10 million home-based businesses in the United States today and, of these, more than thirty percent are owned and operated by women. These figures have been substantiated by an AT&T study, as well as by the U.S. Department of Labor.

Starting a home-based business has provided an opportunity for many people who might otherwise never have the chance to become entrepreneurs.

For others, a home-based business is the ticket out of the world of the urban commuter. In fact, a home-based business is the perfect way to try something new to see how it works while still working another job to pay the bills. Once the business has proven itself and is realizing a profit, you can leave the job to devote full time to your new venture.

Couples often find that investing time and energy in building a business together at home develops stronger relationships in addition to increasing joint income. For the retired and for those with physical disabilities, it is a path to staying involved, exploring self-sufficiency and guaranteeing a profitable future.

Start-Up Steps Never Change

As with any new business, whether located at home or in a commercial location, it is important to follow the basic guidelines for start-up, including conducting a market survey, drawing up a business plan, setting goals, reviewing capital needs and projected income, developing an advertising campaign and establishing a professional image.

However, many businesses, especially in the area of service, can easily be set up in the home, offering a number of advantages for the beginning business owner.

Setting up your business at home automatically eliminates up to seventy-five percent of the start-up costs and responsibilities required for an office or storefront operation. You are, in your home, already making rent or mortgage payments and paying for telephone service, insurance and utilities.

At bare minimum, a commercial location will require $10,000 just to open the doors with basic equipment. In addition, valuable time and energy is saved because you don't have to scout for the location, have utilities installed, or decorate the premises.

Getting Your Feet Wet

A home-based business gives you the opportunity to test the waters with a minimum of risk. This is especially beneficial to first-time entrepreneurs, who may prefer to learn and grow with the business in the comfort of home without the pressures that operating out of a commercial location often brings.

As a hedge against inflation, the home-based business is a natural. In addition to low start-up, tax deductions for use of home as office and business expenses provide relief from a seemingly endless outflow of cash spent on mortgage or rent payments. You must, however, be aware of the tax laws, which allow deductions only for that part of the home "used exclusively and regularly" for business and, as of last year, limited to a modified net income of the business.

After the business is running smoothly, you will find that the potential to earn money is greater because of reduced overhead. Your production will increase because you have more control over your schedule and fewer of the typical interruptions that arise in a commercial setting. Generally, home-based entrepreneurs claim that an added benefit is reduced stress, despite the fact that they are working long hours.

Of course, as with any business arrangement, there are also disadvantages to setting up your business in your home. By recognizing them, however, it is possible to address and minimize the problems before they come up.

Getting to Work

One of the biggest problems faced by home-based entrepreneurs is being able to establish a productive work schedule. There are different types of interruptions that come up in a home environment, including visits from friends and neighbors, household chores that need to be done, the temptation of television and the daily paper when there is work to be produced and the fact that there is no one around to spur you on.

A helpful suggestion for getting down to work is to dress in the morning as if you were going out to a regular job. This alone will help you set your priorities for the day.

The best solution, however, is to establish regular working hours from the onset (although you do have the flexibility as a home-based business owner to arrange your schedule around the times when you are the most productive). If friends want to visit, politely explain to them that you are operating a business which requires your full concentration and arrange a suitable time to get together according to your schedule.

It is also important, if you have family, that they are supportive and willing to arrange their lives as much as possible around your schedule. This can be dealt with through frequent family discussions about what you are doing and how the business operates.

Another difficult area is learning to separate business and pleasure. A home-based business often makes it very easy to work day and night on a project. Again, it is important to allot time for personal activities. The secret to remember is that the work will get done much more efficiently if you are relaxed and rested.

If at all possible, have the business set up in a separate room or area that can be closed off from your personal living space after working hours. In this way, you will be less inclined to take care of some little business detail just because you happen to see it staring you in the face from the kitchen table.

Home-based business owners often experience feelings of isolation from those in their industry. One way to eliminate this is to join local groups, such as the Chamber of Commerce and networking groups, and, at least, to attend the meetings.

Check to see how many members are entrepreneurs, which will give you a built-in support system. By making yourself available to serve on committees, you will also be able to reach further into the community and publicize your business for the cost of your involvement.

The Disadvantages of a
Home-Based Business

- Success is based 100% on your efforts
- Difficulty in establishing solid work habits
- Difficult to know how to set competitive rates
- Limited support system
- Isolation
- Limited work space
- Disruption of personal life
- Clients are uncomfortable coming to your home
- Zoning restrictions

Review Your Local Laws

Before getting started, it is important to check that zoning ordinances in your area will allow you to use your home for business purposes. Since zoning ordinances vary from city to city and county to county, it is necessary to contact the Planning Department of your regional government offices or talk with your attorney to find out what is allowed, based on the type of business, the area to be used within your home, noise control, tax regulations, business signs and other aspects, as well as if you need a special permit or license to operate.

If you are expecting clients to visit your home for business, it is best to have a separate room set up as an office so that when they do come to discuss a job, they won't feel as if they are intruding on a family. If, however, an office is out of the question, make sure you arrange meetings during times when the family is away from home to ensure that there will be no interruptions.

Another option is to go to the client's location when you must have meetings. Depending on the business, however, and the quality of your work, client discomfort shouldn't be a major problem, according to a number of home-based business owners we have interviewed.

God gives every bird its food, but he does not throw it in the nest.

J. G. Holland

As an example, the number of home-based typesetting services has increased dramatically over the past few years and we have never heard of any complaints or problems in this area. The bottom line, as far as the customer is concerned, is still—and will always be—reliable service or high quality products and the knowledge that they are dealing with a professional.

If your business is suited to being home based, it is an option that warrants exploration. The benefits to the beginning entrepreneur can mean the difference between working for someone else or turning a dream into reality.

The key elements, as with any business, are motivation, a needed product or service, careful planning, and the desire to succeed. But sometimes, just knowing that the expenses of establishing a business in a commercial location are alleviated by setting up a home-based enterprise is enough to push you forward to success, one small step after another. ■

Review

If setting up my business at home, I have:

- Checked with the City and County offices in my area regarding required licenses and permits and zoning regulations for home-as-office.
- Set aside a room or an area in my home that will be used exclusively for my business.
- Had a separate telephone installed and have purchased an answering machine or contracted with a message service.
- Set up a separate business bank account.
- Informed friends and family of my business routine and specific working hours to reduce interruptions and distractions.

If setting up in a commercial location, I have:

- Investigated rental rates for the area I am interested in.
- Checked traffic flow, parking and foot-traffic around my proposed location.
- Determined that my business is compatible with others in the area.
- Talked with my prospective landlord about improvements, maintenance, and rent increases.
- Had my lawyer check the rental agreement and any local zoning regulations.
- Secured the necessary operating licenses and permits from the City and/or County.

Notes

Key Points

_____

_____

_____

_____

Possible Locations

_____

_____

_____

_____

_____

_____

Size and Floor Plan Considerations

_____

_____

_____

_____

_____

8

Figuring Costs and Filling in Charts

Having decided that you are ready and able to accept the challenge of starting your own business, it is necessary to take a look at your overall financial picture. Even if you have a healthy savings account, or feel you can start your business with a minimal capital investment, diagnosing your personal financial situation will help you determine on-going expenses.

The easiest way to estimate exactly how much money you will need to get your business started and to cover expenses, including personal living expenses, for the first six months is to prepare a *Cost of Living* or *Cash Flow Statement* and a *Projected Expense Chart*. Samples are provided on the following pages for your use.

Preparing the *Projected Expense Chart* will give you a fairly accurate picture of what it will cost to open the doors and indicate how much income you must generate to realize a profit. The other advantage of creating these charts early in the game is that when you do find that you want to explore funding options, you will already have two of the required documents prepared and will only need to update them.

The first step in examining your financial situation is to ask yourself the following questions:

1. Do I generally pay my bills on time or wait until my creditors start sending me collection notices?
2. Have I regularly reconciled my bank statement so I know how much money I have in my checking account at any given time?

3. Is my philosophy "If I've got it, I spend it" or do I typically carefully plan how I am going to use my income?
4. Have I ever developed a personal budget so I know how much money is coming in, how much is going out and what I have left over?

These are important aspects of your financial personality that will be helpful to understand when running your business. As your business and subsequent involvement with financial matters grows, it will be vital that you have a handle on your philosophy about money. And there is no time like the beginning, when your business concept is being formed, to start learning.

The Cash Flow Statement

Using the chart on Page 75, you can determine your personal living expenses for the past three to six months to help you gauge what you will need to survive during the early stages of your business.

The easiest way to complete the statement is to use your checkbook register, if you write checks for most purchases, and/or cash receipts and copies of money orders as research tools. If your expenses are relatively consistent from month to month, you should be able to get an overview by analyzing one month. A more accurate picture will emerge if you break down income and expense for three to six months to account for periodic payments, such as taxes, insurance and seasonal spending.

Using the samples provided, fill in the amounts in each category from your checkbook register or receipts. Use a separate sheet for every month that you are analyzing. For miscellaneous spending, a standard calculation is five percent of monthly income. Add up each month's expenses, total them all and then divide that figure by the number of months you are analyzing. This will give you an average month expense figure.

Follow the same procedure for income. You can then subtract your expenses from your income to see where you stand. If you have computed your figures accurately, you might run across a few surprises. It isn't unusual to discover that we spend more money than we realize, often on miscellaneous, unneeded purchases. You may be able to see some areas where you can cut back.

The main point, however, is that you now know:

1. How much or whether you can afford to invest your own money in your new business, and
2. What it costs you to live comfortably, which will help you set income goals for the business.

Start-Up Costs

Every business owner has specific standards about how they want to run their operation. One person may feel perfectly comfortable waiting until they are making a profit to order business cards. Another wouldn't dream of opening the doors without cards, brochures and letterhead already printed.

You will have your own ideas about what you need before opening your business. Then, you must find out what it will cost and, if at all possible, prepare the *Start-Up Statement* as indicated in this section.

It is also advisable to figure how much it will cost to run the business for three to six months, using the sample *Projected Expense Forecast* which follows. A six-month projection should give you the opportunity to start getting an idea of what your profits will be down the line.

Cash Flow Statement
Month Of _____

Income		Expenses	
Wages	$_____	Rent or mortgage	$_____
Miscellaneous	_____	Auto loan	_____
		Gas & car repairs	_____
TOTAL	$_____	Auto insurance	_____
		Life insurance	_____
		Medical insurance	_____
Savings	_____	Homeowners insurance	_____
		Taxes	_____
		Loan payments	_____
Credit Line	$_____	Food: At home	_____
		Food: Dining out	_____
		Telephone	_____
Home Equity	$_____	Utilities	_____
		Household repairs, etc.	_____
		Medical bills	_____
		Credit card payments	_____
		Interest expense	_____
		Clothing/dry cleaning	_____
		Travel	_____
		Miscellaneous	_____
		Savings	_____
		TOTAL	$_____

Preparing the *Start-Up Statement* and *Projected Expense Forecast* involves conducting some research. For example, to estimate the cost of business cards or letterhead stationery, contact several printers or copy shops in your area and obtain quotes. Call the local newspaper for prices on different types of ads, including display and classified.

An insurance agent will be able to give you an estimate on liability coverage. Check with the telephone company for information and rates on installing a phone line.

You can also start to shop around to find the best prices on office supplies, equipment and materials needed to conduct business.

After you have completed your research, incorporate the information on the blank charts. Obviously, some of your figures, such as those for telephone expense and taxes, will be "guesstimated." However, the final figure will give you a good idea of how much it is going to cost to get your business up and running for at least six months.

Have the sample chart on page 78 enlarged at your local copy shop if you are planning to use it as part of your Business Plan (See Chapter 13). Enlarging it will cost you a few cents, but using it can save you many dollars in the long run, because of the increased awareness of your financial picture.

Utilizing the same theory, you can develop a *Projected Income Statement*, drawing from industry figures available through your trade association.

This would include all income realized from cash sales, collection of outstanding invoices, credit card sales and miscellaneous income. By subtracting your total expenses from total income, you will get a clear picture of projected profit or loss.

All of these statements will be requested by loan officers, venture capitalists and the Small Business Administration (SBA) if and when you apply for a loan. They require this kind of paperwork to ensure that you have basic business knowledge and a commendable track record, and are serious about

Start-Up Costs

Furniture: Purchase price $_____

                    Down Payment required $_____

Fixtures: Purchase price   _____

                    Down Payment required   _____

Equipment: Purchase price   _____

                    Down Payment required   _____

Installation and delivery costs   _____
Decorating & Leasehold Improvements   _____
Deposits: Utilities and Rent   _____
Fees: Legal, Accounting, Consulting, etc.   _____
Licenses & Permits   _____
Starting inventory   _____
Supplies   _____
Printing   _____
Pre-Opening Advertising & Promotion   _____
Miscellaneous   _____

                 TOTAL start-up expense $_____

                 Less available start-up capital $_____

                 TOTAL amount needed $_____

Projected Expense Statement

Months:	1st	2nd	3rd	4th	5th	6th
Rent						
Utilities						
Telephone						
Insurance						
Professional Services						
Taxes & Licenses						
Advertising						
Office Supplies						
Office Equipment						
Inventory						
Business auto expense						
Travel expense						
Entertainment						
Dues & subscriptions						
Salaries						
Owner's draw						
Loan payments						
Interest payments						
Miscellaneous						
TOTAL						

your venture. You will also be required to fill out a personal financial statement, available through the lending institution, especially if you are the sole owner or a general partner in the business.

Starting on a "Shoestring"

As you saw with the profit/loss statement, start-up costs for a telemarketing business can vary, depending on:

1. How much time and money you want to commit.
2. How fast you want to grow.
3. What your product requires.

One of the most attractive aspects of the telemarketing business is that it is possible to start a one-person operation for under $500, using an existing phone line and telephone.

If you plan to limit the scope of the business to local telemarketing only—perhaps selling subscriptions to a neighborhood newspaper or promoting the services of an area pest control service, for example—the initial start-up expense will be even less: strictly the monthly service charge on your telephone, plus advertising and incidental expenses.

However, to ensure profits, a telemarketing service bureau should be equipped to handle outgoing and incoming calls nationally and, at bare minimum, on a statewide level. You are not likely to get heavy-weight clients if your calling power is limited to the city and three surrounding counties.

Major corporations typically hope that their market is worldwide. If you can at least offer them access to an audience in the continental United States, they will be much more enthusiastic about signing on for service.

As an independent service, it is assumed that you will be selling products and services that will be housed, distributed and/or delivered by your client, thereby eliminating any inventory expenses. This, alone, is a tremendous savings since companies selling a proprietary product must often spend thousands of dollars on production, storage and fulfillment (shipping and handling, for example) costs just to be ready when they start selling via telemarketing. ■

9

Telephone Equipment

One of your most vital capital or start-up expenses will be your telephone equipment. You probably already have a basic telephone system and it may be possible to upgrade it to ensure that you have the most efficient tool for the job. Be aware that if a system is more than five years old, it will probably cost you more to upgrade this 'old' technology than to start again from scratch.

Before heading out for your local phone store, review the following list of features or system enhancements that will not only make the actual job of telemarketing easier, but will help you keep expenses to a minimum, work for you in the development of billing and, after you hire telephone reps down the line, monitor their performance without interrupting momentum.

You should also be aware that telephone systems can be leased or purchased. The decision should be based on several factors including:

1. Available capital versus the overall cost of the system,
2. Expansion plans and goals,
3. How quickly the technology is changing to meet those goals, and
4. Resale value of your system versus the credit on used equipment that the leasing company will guarantee toward purchasing a system.

You will undoubtedly be investigating *key* or *terminal-based systems*, which can accommodate one, two or as many as twenty lines without requiring expensive PBX (private branch exchange) switching capabilities to process incoming and outgoing calls. In a terminal-based system, each telephone has options built in, which is cost-effective if you are dealing with only a few stations.

A *hybrid system* is a cross between a key system and a PBX and would allow you to expand easily in a number of complex configurations to handle fast growth. Some options will be built in to individual stations, which others will be handled directly by the servicing telephone company.

Check Out the Features

Most important, however, are the system enhancements which can make your job easier and provide your clients with more comprehensive service. These include the following features:

1. *Speed dialing.* Cuts dialing time, especially useful when dealing with long-distance carrier access codes.
2. *Touch tone dialing.* A definite necessity in telemarketing and has become a standard feature in most systems.
3. *Conferencing.* A three-way calling device which can also be used to monitor telemarketing reps.
4. *Numeric display.* A digital display showing the number being called on an outgoing basis or an incoming extension to ease routing.
5. *Automatic Call Distributors (ACD).* ACDs process incoming or outgoing calls very quickly and efficiently. These computerized devices are most cost effective when you have 15 or more lines in use on a consistent basis. The points you should check out in ACDs include recordkeeping of calls made from individual telephones, backup operation in the event of a power outage and internal switching capabilities.

6. *Automatic Recorded Message (ARM)*. Although they are still considered controversial as a telemarketing tool, ARMs can be extremely cost-effective when a specific telephone presentation is to be made, i.e., a political message or an insurance company name change being relayed to a group of policy owners.

7. *Wide Area Telecommunications Service (WATS)*. Available for outgoing and certain incoming calls, WATS lines are rented by long-distance carriers based on hours of usage, location of calls (known as zones or bands) and a variety of other factors. Discounts are given for volume calling. The main disadvantage is the high cost for additional lines. Shop carefully.

8. *800 Service.* There are a number of 800 variables available, including the 800 single number service, 800 customized routing when you have more than one branch office handling incoming calls and 800 courtesy response, which gives callers an automatic recorded message when you are closed. The 800 Readyline from AT&T is specifically designed for small companies that want to add an incoming 800 line to an existing system. Check with your long distance carrier for other 800 services.

Do Your Research

There are so many options available to telemarketing service bureaus these days—with new ones being developed every day —that it will be quite simple to custom-design a system to suit your exact needs. The best way to ensure you get tailored equipment and features is to talk to as many companies as possible and ask lots of questions so you can make an informed decision.

Never accept the first offer that comes along . . . telephone companies have become extremely competitive and it is likely that the next one you talk to will have a more comprehensive service package they can put together for you at a better price!

Another important area of consideration is service charges and installation fees; these include fees for setting up the all-important telephone lines. Although installation and service charges vary greatly depending on the city and state where your business is located, the following chart will give you an idea of what to expect.

We encourage you, again, to call several long-distance telephone companies, which include MCI, TMC, SPRINT, and AT&T. Check under *Telephone —Long Distance Carriers* in the Yellow Pages for their specific rates. Those outlined on the following page are based on 1989 AT&T rates for incoming and outgoing lines established in the State of California. Further explanation of the types of telephone lines indicated is provided in this chapter.

An Actual Set-Up

To set up one incoming 800 number *plus* one WATS line that would give you access to all 50 states would cost you approximately the following (*if* you live in California and get your service through AT&T):

- One-time installation charges, approximately $463 (which includes $97.50 + $365.50—see chart on page 85)
- Basic monthly service charges, $68.70 ($20 + $48.70)
- Charges for calls made or received would be based on the specific number of hours you use the service (the actual minutes are accumulated automatically by the telephone company) each month. In addition, you might be charged a "mileage sensitive rate" based on the distance involved, for example, calls made to New York will have a different rate than those made to your neighboring state.

Estimated Charges
(Courtesy of AT&T)

Intrastate (within California)

Incoming 800 Line

Local telephone company set-up	$75 one-time
Local monthly service	$20 monthly
Calling rate	5¢ per call
AT&T Accumulative charges	
(total actual hours per month)	$13.62 per hour of use

Outgoing WATS Line

Local telephone company set-up	$75 one-time
Local monthly service	$25 monthly
Calling rate	13¢ per call
AT&T Accumulative charges	
(total actual hours per month)	$9.05 (up to 15 hours)
	$8.48 (16-40 hours)
	$7.51 (41-80 hours)
	$6.50 (80+ hours)

Interstate (nationwide)

Incoming 800 Line

AT&T installation	$ 97.50 one-time
Monthly service charge	$ 20.00 monthly
Accumulative charges (average)	$ 14.50 hourly

Outgoing WATS Dedicated Line

AT&T installation	$365.50 one-time
Monthly service charge	$ 48.70 monthly
Accumulative charges	30¢ first 20 seconds
	2¢ each add'l 6 sec.

Actually, the total monthly charges could remain as low as $200 or can skyrocket into the thousands, depending on the hours and the distances involved. In many cases, telemarketing service bureaus arrange billing systems that ensure the client picks up a portion of the telephone expense over and above any retainer and/or commissions. We will cover this more completely in Chapter 16, Pricing for Profits.

When conducting your research into installation charges and rates, call as many telephone companies as possible and don't be afraid to ask questions. Also, have them send you any and all literature they have available on the various service packages and rates. Soon the terminology of telephone systems will become old hat.

And There's More . . .

Finally, before signing up with any telephone service company, get all the details on the following:

1. *Monthly billing.* Do they break out the calls by time, date and area code so you can review telephone costs and monitor individual telephone representatives? Is billing for a call based on when the call begins, when it starts ringing, or at the point the call is answered? Are there discounts for volume calling? Surcharges for credit card calls?

2. *Dialing requirements.* Up until recently, the majority of long distance carriers required that a six- to eight-digit code number be dialed in addition to the area code and telephone number being called. This is time-consuming, especially if you are planning on making a specific number of calls per hour, and not very cost-effective. It can also be extremely annoying to dial all those numbers only to find that the line is busy. Check whether the long-distance carrier has speed dialing or equal access features available.

3. *Telephone Line Quality.* If you are unable, for any reason, to test out the quality of the transmission lines at the supplier's office, find out the names of several companies in your area who use the service. Call them and ask if they are satisfied that transmissions are loud and clear with no static or glitches. This is extremely important. If the prospective customer on the other end of the line can't hear you properly, you can count on losing sales.

As you start doing your research, you will run into computerized features, beyond the ACDs and the PBX equipment, which make the business of telemarketing even more efficient.

Although some of these features may seem expensive at first glance, it is important to analyze the long-term benefits, especially in increased productivity.

Considering Computers

For example, if you see your company expanding within the first year to accommodate five or six heavy-duty clients, you must certainly be prepared to have some of the time-consuming record keeping tasks automated. Get information on how computerization can handle such tasks as the following:

1. *Product Information.* With a keystroke, a telephone representative is able to call up specific details on any aspect of the product or service they are selling. Within seconds after a customer brings up a question, or in a natural, scripted sequence, the information appears on a computer screen set up at each rep's station. By the same token, an *Objection File* can be established so the rep simply hits a key and is presented with a screen-full of rebuttals to any customer objection.

2. *Order Fulfillment.* The telephone representative is able to create all of the documents needed to fulfill an order, from sales invoice, packing slip and shipping label to service orders and updating of inventory records. In addition, there are programs which automatically target client files for follow-up at a later date. This not only serves as confirmation of satisfaction, but also provides an opportunity to introduce another product or service.

3. *Activity Reports and Summaries.* Daily, weekly and monthly activity can be recorded automatically to create spreadsheets for monitoring individual reps' performance, and to prepare forecasts.

4. *List Management.* In most cases, reps are calling people from a list of names that has been rented from a list broker or created by your client from responses to advertising, previous sales, etc. If computerized, the lists can be organized according to zip or area codes for timely calling, can be updated easily and even used to print mailing labels.

There are many different computers on the market and it would pay you to talk with dealers who handle the major lines, such as Macintosh, IBM and any others recommended by your long-distance carrier. The main things to look for in a computer system are:

- Compatibility with the telephone system you have decided will suit your purposes
- A minimum of two floppy disk drives
- A central processing unit with 256K of Random-Access Memory (internal memory)
- 64K of Read-Only Memory
- Complete instructions for use
- Telecommunications, database, and word processing software
- Monitor (or screen)

- Printer
- An internal or external 1200-baud telephone modem

Again, sales representatives at your local computer store will be able to introduce you to the best system to suit your needs.

More on Updated Technology

Use hardware and software that can be serviced locally. Unless you know a great deal about computer technology, buy versatile pre-packaged software rather than software that requires customizing. Applications software includes word processing, database management, financial spreadsheet computations, and telecommunications capability. Your software must be compatible with your hardware.

Your basic system (a personal computer, software, and printer), will probably cost somewhere between $2,000 and $10,000 depending on brands and models chosen. If you want your computer to fulfill a variety of functions such as word processing, budgeting, maintaining lists and working with a modem to send electronic mail, you may want to buy an integrated software package that does these tasks simultaneously.

When shopping for an integrated software package, compare your needs with the capabilities of the various packages. Packages strong in some features will be weak in others.

Your accounting software will enable you to keep track of your time and expenses. There are a variety of good time accounting and billing systems available that will allow you to record fee charges, expenses, payments, credits, retainers, and time allotted to each account.

The appropriate software can enable you to organize your records, print statements in a variety of formats and produce internal reports for your company. These packages provide passwords for file security, offer individualized or group billing options, and enable you to monitor client billing, payment history, 30/60/90 day aging information, sales tax on services, and finance charges on past-due accounts.

As discussed above, the type of equipment you purchase is largely dependent on the range of services you offer. From the at-home bank of telephones to the full fledged, state of the art computer system, your equipment depends on need.

Fortunately for you, the entrepreneur, this is one business you can start small and build in sophistication as you go. You may want to go ahead and invest in the most advanced equipment made, but if it is beyond what you consider to be a comfortable expenditure, there are many options.

The least expensive way to get started is to lease or buy equipment and a system and have them installed in your home or work space. The net cost of this depends on the number of clients you see yourself acquiring in the next four to eight months. You can, however, begin with as few lines as you need and build on.

Supplies of Inventory

Because your business is a service business, your product is efficiency and dependability. Supplies and inventory that can help in this regard are the following.

Contracts and Sign-Up Materials

Calling on clients and presenting a case for providing them with service relies mostly on your own ability to be a good representative of that service. A brochure listing the services you offer, printed contract forms and additional materials that help you sell, such as business cards, are also good ideas when it comes to making a professional presentation. You can get all of these items created and printed very reasonably through a desktop publisher and a quick-copy shop, sometimes found in the same location.

You will need office furniture to start your business. Whenever possible buy used furniture. The work area should accommodate your telephone system, presentation materials, computer equipment and/or documentation for manual entry of orders.

If you have more than two telemarketing reps working at any one time, it is important that they have separate stations or cubicles to guarantee concentration. It may be possible to find a carpenter who will build your work stations for less than it would cost to buy modular setups through an office furniture store. Check around . . .you could save a large amount of money.

An absolute must for your reps is headsets. This will free up their hands for writing, using a computer keyboard or, as is common among people who sell, for emphasizing what they are saying with hand gestures—even if nobody sees, it is often the only way some people can talk.

Headsets range in price from $20 for a basic plug-type earphone to $100 for finely-tuned equipment with volume control, mute buttons for privacy and padded microphone to modulate the voice and keep out distracting background noise. A worthwhile investment!

You may want to keep a typewriter handy for quick business correspondence or for typing forms, although a computer can handle all of these tasks. The benefit of a typewriter is you don't have to wait for material to print out; the drawback is that you do not have a permanent record of your copy on disk. Despite all that, you can get a good electric typewriter from $200 to $1,000 depending on whether you buy it used or new.

The following is a list of major equipment and supplies needed for your telemarketing service bureau:

Item	Range		
Telephone system	$ 50	-	$ 5,000
Headsets	20	-	300
Personal Computer	2,000	-	9,000
Software	300	-	2,000
Printer	300	-	700
Modem	200	-	800
Typewriter	200	-	1,000
Calculator	20	-	50
Office supplies	200	-	400
File Cabinets	50	-	300
Office Furniture	300	-	600
TOTALS	**$3,640**	-	**$20,150**

You will want appropriate telephone books and an area code handbook for little towns as well as large cities. These are available at a nominal cost through the Yellow Page Directory company or AT&T, if there is a local office.

There is almost no reason why you should pay high prices for office and working supplies. While doing research for this book, we checked out office supply discount stores and wholesale catalogs and watched for sales. We found that everything needed to outfit your office can be purchased for at least fifty percent under standard retail prices.

In addition to any equipment purchases you decide to make, there is a range of office supplies you'll go through regularly, as follows:

- stapler and staples
- staple remover
- stamp pads and ink

- file folder labels
- cellophane tape
- stamp moistener

- pencils
- electric pencil sharpener
- erasers
- lots of ball point pens
- desk calendars
- wall calendars
- paper clips
- 3x5 index cards
- manila folders,
  letter or legal size
- index tabs

- rubber fingertips
- notepads
- memo holders
- writing paper
- envelopes
- telemarketing forms
  (pre-printed or self-designed)
- letter opener
- typewriter ribbons
- typing correction fluid
- type cleaner

You can request catalogs from these four companies, which offer their products at substantial savings:

Quill Corporation
100 S. Schelter Rd.
Lincolnshire, IL 60069-4700

Colwell Systems, Inc.
201 Kenyon Rd.
P.O. Box 4025
Champaign, IL 61820-1325
(for business forms & stationery)

HG Professional Forms Co.
2020 California Street
Omaha, NE 68102

General Wholesale Products
2957 E. 46th St.
Los Angeles, CA 90058
(for office equipment, files, etc.)

Because many mail-order companies make their lists available to other suppliers, before too long you'll find yourself getting more catalogs than you'll ever need. ■

Notes

Key Points

_____

_____

_____

_____

Equipment Needs

_____

_____

_____

_____

_____

Possible Suppliers

_____

_____

_____

_____

_____

10

Selecting Professionals

From the start-up stage and as your business continues to grow and prosper, you will need the assistance of several professionals, including a lawyer, an accountant and an insurance agent.

The best way to find a professional, according to the majority of business owners, is through personal recommendations from other entrepreneurs, especially those in similar businesses as yours, and from friends or relatives. The most important factor is that the person doing the recommending understand exactly what you will need from the professional you will be hiring.

For example, your cousin's divorce lawyer is probably not as well suited to helping you draw up a partnership agreement as the attorney who helped your friends incorporate their business.

Before making a decision, talk to several recommended professionals until you find someone who can best satisfy your needs for the business as outlined below and who has a fee structure you can afford. Equally important is that it be someone whom you feel comfortable with, especially during those times when you are forced by external forces to call five times a week to resolve a problem or complete a specific task. In many cases, because attorneys and accountants often work on a particular business matter in conjunction with one another, the attorney you select may be able to suggest an accountant who can properly serve your business, or vice-versa.

If you are planning to hire an attorney or an accountant, you should start "interviewing" likely candidates eight to nine months prior to the date you plan to start the business. This will give you time to find a suitable match, and give them time to take care of all start-up functions, such as establishing your business form and helping you with your business plan.

What to Expect from Professional Services

Legal

You will need an attorney with broad-based expertise in business who can help you with such matters as raising capital; the legal and tax ramifications and benefits of various business forms including sole proprietorship, partnership or corporation; name clearance to insure that you are not using a name already designated by another company; legal tips on operating in your desired location; and the ability to file all necessary legal papers and documents needed for financing, establishing your business form and so on.

He or she will review contracts and lease agreements, and can provide support with collection problems. The lawyer you select should also be willing and able to represent you in the event of any claims that are brought against you or lawsuits you initiate.

Another crucial area of concern are the rules and regulations that govern telecommunications in general and telemarketing, specifically. The attorney you choose to work with should be well-versed in these laws—some of which are outlined on the following few pages—or must be able, at bare minimum, to gain quick access to the federal and state codes that govern the specific areas of your business.

Telemarketing Legalities

Credit Card Fraud

Credit cards have revolutionized buying and the majority of what you are selling for your clients will probably involve credit card purchasing. Many telemarketers claim that if they get a credit card sale, they consider it a much more secure transaction than if the prospect offers to send in a check. And, in many cases, this is sound reasoning—people typically forget to mail the check.

However, you must be aware of the high incidence of credit card fraud in this country. In fact, the U.S. Office of Consumer Affairs estimates it will exceed one billion dollars in the next two years. The best way to prevent the problem from affecting your profit goals is to make sure you and your telemarketing representatives take precise steps each time a credit card is involved in a sale.

You can get a directory from most of the major cards that lists issuing banks and, in conjunction, most credit cards have a Business Identification Number (BIN) stamped on the face. Always check the directory to make sure the card and the BIN match. In addition, request regularly updated listings of bad or expired cards, which should also be checked.

You will eventually start to compile your own in-house list, unfortunately, of individuals and businesses you do not want to deal with because of credit card problems. Your reps are likely to encounter suspicious or even obviously fraudulent situations.

If using a list from a reputable list broker, the name and address of the prospect will generally be listed along with the telephone number. Make it a point to ask the credit card user to give *you* their address and work phone number, rather than verifying, e.g., "Is your address still 123 Apple Lane?"

Your lawyer as well as your bank manager will have additional tips on ways to prevent credit card fraud from ruining an otherwise perfect day.

These include everything from a call-in credit card approval following each sale, to making sure that the reps you hire have solid backgrounds indicating a reliable, honest work history.

A Few More Specifics

The growth of telemarketing has created a number of other legal hotspots and the laws pertaining to these potential problems must be adhered to if you plan to stay in business.

Although your lawyer will be able to fill you in on the details of Federal Communications Commission (FCC) rulings affecting interstate telecommunications and on Public Utilities Commission regulations for your state, you should ask for information on the specific aspects that follow.

Profit Disclosure affects fundraising efforts and requires that public reports be made available on the amount of donations that go toward promotion, telemarketing and administrative versus the actual amount going to the charity. Although the responsible party would be your client—a charity or nonprofit organization that hires you to handle the telemarketing—you should check to see if your state currently has regulations on the books or is planning to enact such rulings at some point in the near future.

Registration by telemarketers is required by the government in many states. This has happened because of the great numbers of unscrupulous telemarketing operations that periodically spring up offering free trips, gifts and other inducements to unsuspecting prospects. Check with your state Attorney General's Office for registration requirements.

Calling hours are strictly monitored in most areas to ensure that the public is not unduly bothered. In most cases, the laws can be automatically adhered to if you simply use common sense. For example, although many people are home on a Saturday morning, some like to sleep in.

The logical thing to do would be to start making calls at about 10 a.m. on a Saturday. The inherent advantage is that you are less likely to run across grouchy prospects who just hang up the phone on you anyway. Have your attorney check, regardless, to see if there are solicitation rulings in your state.

Homeowners are protected under state and federal *home solicitation laws,* which provide them with legal support in the event of fraud, deception or theft. The laws cover obscenity, harassment and false representation as well. They also require telemarketers to clearly announce their name, company or product name and reason for calling. Basically, it means that you and your reps must be honest, direct, and polite.

The U.S. Department of Justice codes pertaining to home solicitation laws (under Title 18 and Title 15 of the U.S. Code) should be included in any training programs you provide, along with the legislation dealing with consumer product safety, and consumer credit protection. A well-advised team of telemarketers will be a profitable and long-term team.

Your attorney should also be able to provide you with information on rulings or pending legislation dealing with call monitoring—even when you are using it strictly as a training tool—and the recently initiated asterisk bill, which is the addition in telephone directories of an asterisk beside the names of private citizens and companies that do not wish to be contacted by telephone for unauthorized solicitation.

This has already resulted in the Direct Marketing Association (DMA) publishing a Telephone Preference List, or "No-Go" list as it is often called since those listed do not want to be contacted. The list is available to members of the DMA.

The secret to operating your telemarketing service bureau profitably and legally is being aware of the laws governing the industry. This is how membership in one or more of the associations listed in the Resource section at the end of this book will be a benefit.

Regular newsletters should contain updates of regulations that affect telemarketing. Be sure to ask if this is the case when you are considering signing up for membership.

Your next responsibility is to ensure that your telemarketing reps know the rules and abide by them. While it is true that one or two good reps can make you a success, the other side of the coin is that one or two bad apples—dishonest, disrespectful, or basically uncaring—can destroy your credibility.

Keep the bad apples out by careful hiring practices, thorough training, regular meetings, and consistent control on their telephone performances. By following all of these practices, you should have no problem in learning to live with and by the rules and regulations pertaining to telemarketing.

What to Expect in Legal Fees

Depending on your lawyer's expertise, reputation and location (metropolitan area versus small town, for example), fees will differ dramatically. In a smaller community, lawyers often charge a set rate for the job being done while "city" lawyers typically charge by the hour with fees ranging anywhere from $65 to $250 per hour.

This does not include the extraneous expenses involved, such as the $300 to $1,000 cost of incorporating, depending on the state you operate in. Fees also do not include supplemental costs, such as travel and telephone, incurred by the attorney in the handling of your case.

A good way to get an idea of what to expect in the way fees in your area is to check with your local Chamber of Commerce or the state Bar Association, generally located in the capital city. The Bar Association may also be able to provide you with information about a particular attorney's reputation and expertise.

When talking with potential attorneys—and when you have found one who is compatible to your needs—always be sure to ask for an outline of expenses and also find out if they are willing to notify you when the fees for a particular job will be exceeded.

Accounting

The accountant you select should, early on, be able to work with you on putting together your business plan, including your projected profit and loss statements, for financing.

Down the line as your business is being established, the accountant will help you set up your books and, once in operation, should handle your tax returns, prepare financial statements and offer financial advice regarding tax matters, cash flow, investments to maximize the use of profits, and the tax regulations regarding employees, when you are ready to hire.

Projecting the Fees

As with attorneys, there is a professional association in your state capital which certifies and maintains records on the reputation and fee structures of accountants. The basis for fee structuring does vary slightly, however, with accountants. Some charge by the hour, others by the day, and still others work on a set monthly retainer, based on the estimated amount of time they will be required to spend on your work. Hourly fees, however, average between $25 and $100 depending on expertise and location.

Insurance

Before setting out on your search for an insurance agent, it is advisable to have already established your business form and learned exactly what insurance the law in your area requires you to carry (fire, liability, etc.) and, if hiring employees, what kind of program you want to offer your employees, as well as your own needs for medical and life insurance.

There are several types of insurance you should carry for your Telemarketing Business. General Business coverage will protect against fire and theft, General Liability covers accidents or injury to anyone while they are on your work (home) premises, and Product Liability covers against anyone getting hurt somehow with one of your products. If working out of your home, it may be possible to add these additional types of coverage to your existing Homeowners policy at a low annual cost.

You will also need to carry Workman's Compensation when you start hiring full or part-time employees, unless they agree to work as independent contractors and take care of their own insurance and taxes.

The insurance agent you choose should be familiar with the needs of businesses and business owners, not just the standard life and disability policies. Your insurance needs will change as your business grows and expands (i.e., employee health, workman's compensation, etc.). At that point, you may want to consider key-person coverage to make sure your company can survive if a major partner or employee dies.

There are also a number of pension programs and stock-option programs available in the event you want to offer employees the incentive to increase their participation in the company in exchange for partial 'ownership' down the line.

Fees for Insurance Coverage

The fees for your agent's expertise are paid from your premiums, and there should definitely not be any extra charge to you for advice or administration of your insurance policies and programs. ■

11

Taxes, Licenses, and Permits

As a business owner, you are responsible for timely report filing and payment of federal, state and local taxes. Whether you have an accountant prepare your returns, or do it yourself, the task will be made much easier if you establish a systematic record keeping system as reviewed in Chapter 15 and keep your records accurate and up-to-date.

This includes maintaining all written documents pertaining to the financial aspect of your business; invoices, bank statements, receipts of any and all business expenses and deposit slips.

One of the easiest ways to keep control of the "paper dragon" is to set up a 9 x 12-inch manila envelope or a file folder for each of the following categories: *Paid Bills*—both personal and business; *Sales Receipts* of every product you've sold or service job performed; *Inventory* records based on on-going inventory control; *Copies of Invoices* or billing statement that are paid, with a separate file for billing still due you; *Receipts* for miscellaneous cash purchases; *Auto* and *Entertainment* receipts from travel and promotional activities.

All of these documents must be kept for at least five years to substantiate deductions claimed on your income tax returns in the event of an I.R.S. audit. Make up new file folders or envelopes at the beginning of each year and store the old ones in a safe place.

It is not only a time-consuming task that can take you away from the important job of running your business, but preparing income tax returns, especially for the federal government, has become almost an art form. Tax law is a constantly changing, complicated fact of life. It is strongly recommended that you have an accountant lined up to prepare your taxes and keep you informed of any pertinent changes during the year.

Business Deductions

The deductions that you will most likely qualify for as a business owner include expenses incurred for the operating of business, such as telephone, postage, advertising, bank service charges, travel and expense of conventions, interest, dues to professional organizations, and subscriptions to magazines pertaining to your business, among others.

If you have established your business at home, you will be able to deduct that portion of the house used exclusively for business, as well as a percentage of your costs for telephone service and utilities.

Taxes are what we pay for civilized society.

Oliver Wendell Holmes, Jr.

Again, because of the complexity and obscurity of many of the deductions, it is best to have a professional do your taxes to ensure you get the full benefits you are entitled to.

The list on the next page provides an overview of the tax returns which may be applicable to your business situation. It is meant only to inform you. Filing requirements will be determined by the type of business, the legal structure (sole proprietorship, partnership or corporation), income from the business, your location, state and local laws and whether or not you have employees.

For example, as the sole proprietor of your business you would probably only be required to file personal federal and state returns based on profit or loss with the appropriate schedules for business expenses, pay sales, self-employment and estimated taxes and local business license fees and sales tax.

Federal Tax Returns

Form 1040: Income tax for Sole Proprietors,
   Partners or S Corporation shareholders.
Schedule C: Profit (or Loss) from Business or Profession.
Form 1065: Partnership income tax return.
Schedule K-1: Partner's share of Income, Credits,
   Deductions, etc.
Form 1120: Corporation tax return with applicable
   support schedules.
Form 2553: S Corporation Filing.
Form 1120-S: S Corporation Tax Return.
Form 1040ES: Quarterly Estimated Tax for
   Sole Owner or Partner.
Form 1120W: Quarterly Estimated Tax for Corporation.
Form 940: Federal Unemployment (Social Security)
   Tax for Sole Owner, Partner, Corporations.
Schedule SE: Annual return of self-employment tax
   for Sole Proprietor or Partner.

State Income Tax

Each state has corresponding filing requirements. However, form and schedule numbers vary. Contact your State Franchise Tax Board or your accountant for details.

Local Taxes

Taxes will vary from city to city and county to county. However, you *may* be required to pay city income tax, local sales tax as well as real or personal property taxes. Check with your local government offices for specifics.

Licenses and Permits

To operate your business, you will need permits and licenses based on the requirements in your area and the type of business you are running. You will probably, however, be required to obtain the following documents no matter where you live.

Local Business License.   Basically this is simply a fee paid to the city or county in which you are located which allows you to operate your business in that area. Some cities will also require you to pay a percentage of your gross sales every year.

Fictitious Name Statement.   This is a registration for protection of your business name. Filing for the Fictitious Name Statement will also involve a city or county-wide search to make sure you are not duplicating an existing name. See details in Naming Your Business in Chapter 12.

Seller's Permit or Resale Certificate.   This is required only if you are going to be charging sales tax. Services are often exempt.

Health Permit.   This is required only if you are preparing or distributing food in any manner. Involves an initial inspection and periodic follow-up inspections by Health Department officials.

Taxpayer Identification Number, available from the I.R.S. by filing Form SS-4, in the case of partnerships, S Corporations or Corporations. Sole Proprietors are required to have a Taxpayer Identification Number if they pay wages to one or more employees or file pension or excise tax forms.

Your local governmental offices or your attorney will be able to give you specific licenses and permits needed to conduct business in your area.

Legal Structure

As a self-employed business owner, you are required to decide on a legal form of business for tax reporting purposes. There are four basic classifications, as outlined below. If, after reviewing them, you are still unsure of which way to go, it would be advisable to talk with a lawyer about the advantages and disadvantages of each structure for your particular business.

Sole Proprietorship is the easiest to establish and is the structure many small business owners choose. A proprietorship is relatively free from government regulation, as the business has no existence apart from the owner. Profits from the operation of business are treated as personal income for purposes of taxation and your proprietary interest ends when you die or dissolve the business. The major drawback of a proprietorship is that you are personally liable for any and all claims against the business and undertake the risks of the business to the extent of all assets, whether they are used in the business or personally owned. As a sole proprietor, you will be required to file self-employment tax returns and ordinarily would have to make estimated tax payments on a quarterly basis.

A *General Partnership* is also easy to set up and administer. Since responsibilities and capitalization are usually shared by two or more partners, taxation is based on each partner's share of business income and determined by their individual tax rates. Again, claims against the business can be filed against personal assets and financial liability is shared equally by all partners.

A *Limited Partnership* can be established when one or more people are willing to invest cash or tangible property in the business with active participation in the daily operations. However, there must be at least one general partner who carries unlimited financial liability and usually maintains a full-time managerial position within the company.

The limited partner(s) are only liable for business debts up to the amount of their investment. Although a partnership is not a taxable entity, it must figure its profit or loss and file an annual tax return, which also becomes part of the partners' personal returns.

In a *Corporation*, stock or shares in the business are sold to investors or stockholders, who then control the company. The advantage is that corporate stockholders are removed from any liability against personal assets. The most anyone can lose in the event of bankruptcy or a liable claim is their stock.

The privilege of reduced liability, however creates paperwork (Articles of Incorporation and annual reports for the State Tax Commission and federal regulators), expenses (filing and licensing fees) and double taxation (the corporation is taxed on profits, while stockholders and elected officers are taxed individually on wages and/or dividend income).

Subchapter S Corporations have proven to be a real boon for small business owners who want the benefit of corporate protection from personal liability without double taxation. In a Subchapter S Corporation, a maximum of 35 stockholders (who can be family members) report their share of corporate income on individual tax returns.

The corporation itself is generally exempt from federal income tax. However, it may be required to pay a tax on excess net passive investment income, capital gains or built-in gains. To structure your company as a Subchapter S Corporation, all of the shareholders must consent to the choice.

All businesses, regardless of size, are required to maintain detailed records and file the necessary tax returns. In a corporation, regular meetings must be held. The stockholders elect a board of directors, who establish and monitor general corporate policy. The board also selects corporate officers to conduct the day-to-day operations of the business.

Sole Proprietorships are the most convenient and least complicated form of business organizations for new business owners, especially in the early stages. As your business grows, you will want to explore the options as a way of protecting your personal assets and increasing the potential for expansion capital.■

12

Naming Your Business

As a pet owner, it is unlikely that you would give your German shepherd a name like "Fifi." It wouldn't suit the dog's image, nor would it be appropriate. The same principle applies to choosing a name for your business.

The name you select for your business can be a tremendous asset when it defines the kind of image you want to project. You want the name to attract and appeal to potential customers, to be easily remembered over that of the competition's, and appropriate to the type of business you are starting.

Today's consumers are constantly bombarded in advertising as they go about their daily routines with company and product names. Getting their attention, and holding it long enough for them to make an association between your business name and what you are offering, is imperative.

A memorable moniker can mean the difference between continued growth or a mediocre response from an audience victimized by information overload. (It is, of course, important to remember that ultimate success is dependent on well-designed advertising, careful planning, and quality products and/or service.)

Many small business owners claim their image is enhanced by the use of a straightforward name that conveys their business concept but maintains a sense of personal identity—a factor that is especially important in today's hi-tech world.

As an example, when Susan Hopper made the decision to open a preschool in a Southern California community, she grappled with names like The ABC Center, KiddieLand and Now We Are Three. Finally, out of exasperation and because she felt these selections were either inappropriate or too cute, she decided to go with Susan's School, feeling it was easy to remember and conveyed exactly the personal, homey atmosphere she was wanting to create. She claims that fifty percent of the parents who have picked her preschool for their children from the telephone book did so because it sounded friendly and sincere.

Historically, in developing business names, simplicity has scored the highest points. The name you choose should be short, to the point and easy for consumers to pronounce.

If however, you do not want to name the business after yourself, you must be sure that what you do come up with is catchy enough to stand above the rest of the similar businesses in your area. Start by making a list of all the positive aspects of you business that you can think of, and call on friends and relatives to provide as many ideas as they can come up with, also. Take some time to think about this, because your company name needs to fulfill several functions beyond identifying you. The name you choose:

• Can affect a customer's perceptions of your legitimacy.
• Can determine whether or not you have to get a special city, state or county license to operate your business.
• Can affect your ad costs; the shorter the name, the less you pay. And at $4-$8 a word, it adds up.
• Shouldn't be so exclusive that you can't sell other products under the same name when you expand.

All things considered, it is probably best to just use your own name followed by "company," "enterprises," "products" or the like. It leaves room to grow. And, unless your name utilizes every letter in the alphabet more than once, your ad costs will be that much lower.

If, for any reason, you should choose not to use your own name, come up with a name that appeals both to the eye and ear, and keep it general: Associated Enterprises, Bay Area Distributors, Western Products, and so on.

Write down all the possibilities, no matter how funny or unusual they seem. A handy tool for business naming is the thesaurus, which will give you a vast number of options for commonplace names. Consider everything that springs forth from your imagination.

When you have created a list of 15, 25, or more likely candidates, get together with a group of supportive friends and family members and have a brainstorming session to either pick one of the choices you have come up with or to develop something from the ideas listed. Chances are that within a few hours, you will have a name for your business.

Catchy names are fun to design. However, make sure it isn't so off-beat, cute or trendy as to risk slipping into obscurity as time passes. For instance, the astrology craze of the 1970s resulted in thousands of businesses being named after stars, birth signs or related celestial phenomena. As the trend faded, a number of business were able to change their focus *and* their name to survive. Others, however, were so closely associated to their astrological name that they were forced, unfortunately, to close.

. . . And an Address

In addition to choosing a name, you need to decide about an address. There are two schools of thought here. One is that it's preferable to have a post office box rather than use your home address. Boxes are tax deductible, help keep your address short in ads, and keep things simple if you move within the same area.

On the other hand, customers may respond more positively to a street address because it lends a certain sense of trustworthiness. Perhaps in your area there is a private postal box service that provides addresses like, "John Q. Public, 2323 Main Street, Suite 22, Anytown." These are great because they are boxes that look like street addresses. They are, however, more expensive than U.S. Postal Service boxes.

The Fictitious Name Statement

You are required to file a fictitious name statement with the County Clerk's office where you will be basing the business. While there, you should be able to do a county-wide name check on the spot to see if there are any other businesses in the region using the name you have selected. The filing fee is $10 to $20, depending on where you live, and must be done within 30 days after you officially open your business.

It will also be necessary to publish the fictitious name in your local newspaper, which will cost between $25 and $50, depending on the circulation of the paper. The County Clerk's office will advise you about specific requirements in your area.

If you are starting a business that will be operating in a broader market, statewide or nationally, it is important to have your attorney do a name clearance investigation, which can take from three days to three weeks.

Your Visual Image

After you have selected a name that reflects your business image, the next step is translating it into a visual symbol or logo (logotype) to serve as the signature piece for your business. Often this involves creating a visual interpretation of your company name, but in other cases, a graphic symbol or trademark is designed to serve as identification.

Some established corporate trademarks are so familiar that, in many cases, you can immediately identify the company even without seeing or hearing its name.

A good example of this includes the logo of the dog with his head cocked to one side. The accompanying copy reads, "His Master's Voice," and it's a good bet that you recognize this as the logo for RCA. Another effective logo is the avant garde apple that identifies Apple computer products.

If you do not have the graphic skills necessary to design a logo with impact, get in touch with your nearest art association (listed in the phone book or available through local art supply shops or galleries) or call a nearby college or university. Ask the head of the art department if your design can be given as a class assignment or whether they would recommend a student to do the job for a small fee.

It will give students practical application and the design can be used later in their portfolio. You can offer a prize or a fee for the best design and the students will undoubtedly meet the challenge with enthusiasm and give you a number of good samples and ideas from which to choose.

Selecting a Typeface

Save sample logos and advertisements that use a typeface you like. Type, created either by a professional typesetting machine or on a desktop publishing computer, is an extremely important element of logo design and can also pinpoint the precise image you hope to express. Type not only presents the basic message, it can play a powerful role in the overall appearance of your logo and can actually create atmosphere. We have provided a chart on Page 118 of some of the more popular typefaces available.

When deciding on a typeface for your logo, visit print shops or typesetting studios and look at their typeface books. They offer both the usual, functional varieties as well as a selection of unique typefaces that can really dress up your logo by portraying a specific personality such as dignified, fun, feminine, powerful, classic, ultra-modern, etc., in a subtle way.

Have the logo and your business information (address, phone number, etc.) set in more than the one typeface so that you can see how they will look when printed. Also ask to have them set in both small (10-point to 12-point for business cards) and larger (20- to 24-point for letterhead) versions. Once typeset, you will be able to make a final decision about which typeface suits the image you want to project.

Typesetters generally have a minimum fee based on the amount of time they spend on a job and this can vary anywhere from $15 per hour in a small city to $50 per hour in a business area and as high as $100 per hour in major metropolitan areas, so be sure to shop around.

Word processors or independent desktop publishers can also provide a variety of typefaces and formats at less expense. Since you will only be having a few words typeset, the time and cost required to set them in several different styles should certainly be affordable.

Business Cards and Stationery

The typeface and logo you eventually choose will be used on your letterhead, in your display and telephone advertising, on all promotional materials, including flyers, brochures and announcements, on your sign and on statements and invoices.

It will also be used on your business cards, one of the most inexpensive and convenient ways to inform people about your service or product. Once you have had them printed, be generous. Give them to everyone you meet and always be sure to carry a supply wherever you go.

Most fast-print copy centers are prepared to help you if you decide not to design your own business cards and stationery. They have samples of business forms, letterhead and cards with various styles to choose from. Make sure that your company name, logo, address and phone number is included where necessary. When someone looks at your card or letterhead, it must tell them instantly who you are, what your business is, and where they can find you. ■

Sample Typefaces

Helvetica Medium Conden
ABCDEFGHIJKLMNOPQR
abcdefghijklmnopqrstuvwx

Helvetica Black Italic
ABCDEFGHIJKLMNO
abcdefghijklmnopqr

ITC Korinna Medium
ABCDEFGHIJKLM
abcdefghijklmnop

ITC Korinna Bold
ABCDEFGHIJKLM
abcdefghijklmnopq

ITC Korinna Extra Bold
ABCDEFGHIJKL
abcdefghijklmnop

ITC Korinna Heavy
ABCDEFGHIJK
abcdefghijklmn

Melior Roman
ABCDEFGHIJKL
abcdefghijklmno

Melior Italic
ABCDEFGHIJKL
abcdefghijklmno

Melior Bold
ABCDEFGHIJKL
abcdefghijklmno

Linotext Roman
ABCDEFGHIJK
abcdefghijklmnopqrst

ITC Serif Gothic Light
ABCDEFGHIJKLMN
abcdefghijklmnop

ITC Bauhaus Medium
ABCDEFGHIJKLMN
abcdefghijklmnop

ITC Bauhaus Bold
ABCDEFGHIJKLM
abcdefghijklmno

Eurostile Roman
ABCDEFGHIJKL
abcdefghijklmnop

Eurostile Bold
ABCDEFGHIJKL
abcdefghijklmnop

Eurostile Extended
ABCDEFGHIJKL
abcdefghijklmno

Eurostile Extended Bold
ABCDEFGHIJKLM
abcdefghijklmnopq

Helvetica Bold Outline
ABCDEFGHIJKLMNOP
abcdefghijklmnopqrstu

Helvetica Medium Roman
ABCDEFGHIJKLMNOPQ
abcdefghijklmnopqrstuv

Helvetica Bold Italic
ABCDEFGHIJKLMNOP
abcdefghijklmnopqrst

Times Roman
ABCDEFGHIJKL
abcdefghijklmnop

Times Italic
ABCDEFGHIJKLM
abcdefghijklmnopqr

Optima Roman
ABCDEFGHIJKLM
abcdefghijklmnop

Optima Italic
ABCDEFGHIJKLM
abcdefghijklmnop

Optima Bold
ABCDEFGHIJKLM
abcdefghijklmnop

Pabst Extra Bold
ABCDEFGHIJ
abcdefghijklm

Pabst Extra Bold It
ABCDEFGHIJK
abcdefghijklm

Palatino Roman
ABCDEFGHIJKL
abcdefghijklmno

Palatino Italic
ABCDEFGHIJKL
abcdefghijklmnopq

Palatino Bold
ABCDEFGHIJK
abcdefghijklmn

Kuptial Script
ABCDEFGHIJKL
abcdefghijklmnopqrstuu

ITC Tiffany Roman
ABCDEFGHIJK
abcdefghijklmno

ITC Tiffany Heavy
ABCDEFGHIJ
abcdefghijklm

13

Developing a Business Plan

Developing your business plan is the most important process you will undertake in your career as an entrepreneur, regardless of the size or type of business you have decided to start.

A well thought-out business plan will serve as a blueprint while your idea turns into a recognizable entity and as it grows into a stable and profitable venture. Too often we hear former small business owners say they probably could have made a success of their business if they had only known what to expect from the beginning . . . and that is where the business plan comes in.

Unfortunately, too many new entrepreneurs are unfamiliar with the importance of planning or they consider themselves an exception and feel they can succeed by winging it or dealing with problems as they arise. Not so!

Every business, whether a large commercial or a small home-based venture, needs to analyze its potential, examine strengths and weaknesses, and determine the future of the company. It works for the major corporations and it will work for you, especially once you become involved in the day-to-day operations of the business! Having a business plan will give you the freedom to follow the steps you have carefully laid out with regard to budgeting, the success ratio of a product or service, the hiring of employees, and other growth decisions.

The Advantages of Planning

Once you have made the decision to become a business owner, you must devise a specific statement that clearly outlines *what* you plan to do, *when* you plan to do it and *how* you will accomplish the short and long-term goals.

Not only will this keep you on track, it will serve as an indicator of your sincerity and knowledge to others when you go out to find start-up or expansion capital, and as the foundation of your financing proposal.

The other advantage is that the actual task of putting your business plan together will help you define and clarify every step of your concept and, if done in a conscientious and objective manner, will point out potential trouble spots that can be addressed before they become major problems.

If all the necessary components are covered, it will put your business on the road to profit. It is a sure bet that, down the road, if you find your business is not generating the income you had originally projected, this is because you didn't include one or more of the basic business plan requirements.

Not a Guessing Game

Like any other major project, preparing a business plan involves time and research. It shouldn't be a guessing game. It will be necessary to ask yourself some very specific questions and to answer them thoughtfully and honestly. The business plan is your foundation, so build it carefully to insure that it works at optimum efficiency for your needs. And make sure it is typed, orderly, and good looking, so you, and others, recognize its importance in your professional scheme of things.

An important aspect to remember is that your business plan is not cast in stone. In fact, one of the wonderful things about a business plan is that it invites change and revisions as your business changes. This makes it a companion in your success and, by reviewing it regularly, a partner in your progress.

The best way to approach your business plan is to take paper and pen and devote a few hours to coming up with some hard answers. Of course, you will want to condense your answers to fit into specific segments within the plan, including (in order of appearance) Concept and Feasibility, Legal Structure, Product or Service, Customer Base, Marketing and Production Goals, Personnel (your resume and Entrepreneurial Profile and those of any other key personnel), and Financial Statements.

Work Tip

Plan ahead. Allow yourself plenty of time to handle all the tasks involved with marketing a client's product or service.

Set up concise work schedules using weekly and monthly planning calendars and create lists to make sure you do everything that must be done.

It is advisable to start each segment on a separate page and to create a Table of Contents to place in the front. Be sure it is neatly typed, well-written and organized, and bound in a report folder to preserve it and give it a professional quality, especially when using it as a "sales" tool to convince lenders.

Starting to Build Your Business Plan

The first question you must ask yourself is, "Why am I interested in this particular business?" Probably your answer will be something to the effect of wanting to be your own boss and making money . . . Independence and Income.

This answer is fine as a personal goal, but it isn't going to be good enough if you are planning to approach potential lenders for funding. They will want to see an overview of your business concept, why you are convinced it will be successful and where it fits in the scheme of similar businesses in your town or city.

The next question you must address is, "What is my product or service?" This may seem like a ridiculous question since you know your product is gift baskets or your service is catering, local sightseeing tours or whatever, but it goes deeper. Your written response will include details about the service or a description of your product (preferably positive), and focusing on why customers will be inclined to purchase from you.

Additional questions to analyze should include:

- Why do I believe there is a need for my product or service?
- How do I plan to develop my business over the next five years?
- How much will I charge to ensure value to the customer and profit for myself?
- Who are my suppliers?
- Who are my customers?
- What equipment do I need to start the business?
- How much inventory and supplies do I need for start-up?
- What will it cost?
- Who is my competition and where are they located?
- What are they offering and how can I improve my offer to attract customers?
- What changes are occurring in my marketing area which will affect my business in the future?
- What are my estimated sales figures for each of the next five years (a 'guesstimate' based on researching similar businesses in the area)?
- How will I advertise and promote my business (including estimated costs of doing so)?

- What is involved in the production—materials, labor, costs?
- Where will my service be performed?
- What equipment is required for my service (costs for leasing versus purchasing)?
- What are other overhead expenses (rent, employees, etc.)
- How many people will be involved in the business and what are their qualifications?
- If I don't have employees, am I qualified to run the business myself? Will I need outside assistance?

By talking with people in similar businesses, suppliers and direct competitors, as well as your local Chamber of Commerce, you will gather a great deal of information, both positive and the negative, about your potential business. People love to talk about their success and, if you ask in the right way, their failures.

Show me a person with an obsession about succeeding and a solid business plan and I'll show you a good risk.

Anonymous Loan Officer

Become an investigative reporter for a few days while preparing to write your business plan and it's guaranteed that you will obtain plenty of good, solid information. A Service Corps of Retired Executives (SCORE) representative through the Small Business Information can also offer assistance, or give you resources that will help you develop a realistic business plan.

Trade associations, listed in reference books available at your local library, can provide you with invaluable details on industry facts and figures, such as the percentage of gross sales that should be spent on advertising, the percentage that is typically paid for rent in your particular business and how to price your product or service, for example.

The final item to include in this section of your business plan, when and if presenting it for financing, is a personal resumé, designed to emphasize your business management experience, in general, and your expertise within the area of your chosen business, specifically.

Describe the job duties for every job you have held, including any special aspects that pertain directly to the business. If you can not prepare the resumé, it is worth the $25 to $40 to have it done professionally.

The Financial Pages

Once you have written your overview and description sheets, it is time to get down to numbers. This is the key to your business plan and, unfortunately, the area where many entrepreneurs get bogged down. But without an understanding of the numbers involved, you can never expect to be a good manager and really shouldn't be surprised if you run into money problems within the first year.

Again, utilizing the resources indicated above—Chamber of Commerce, trade associations, etc.—you will need to work up your financial pages to include the following components, which most lenders will want to see spread out for between one and five years.

- *Projected operating expenses.* Includes materials, advertising, salaries for employees or outside labor, and other expenses directly related to the cost of doing business.

- *Estimate of gross (before tax) sales revenue.* Based on research figures from trade associations and what the local market dictates, if the business is not yet operating or, if open, how many items or hours of service you plan to sell, and the average price.
- *How you arrived at the figures for these statements.* Generally you would base your figures on assumptions made about the number of months of operation, estimated number of sales, and the average amount versus the cost of each sale.
- *Cost of equipment and furnishings.* Get estimated quotes, whether planning to purchase or lease these items.
- *Cost of materials* for production, if applicable, or maintenance on equipment needed to run the business.
- *Additional operating expenses.* Rent, telephone, and other utilities, business taxes and license fees, office supplies, even decorating costs and a category called "other" to provide a cushion for unexpected expenses.
- *Balance sheet.* Shows assets, such as equipment and operating capital you already have, and liabilities or debts and expenses (if the business has not yet started, this would be a personal balance sheet indicating your net worth; listing all possessions of any value, plus cash, stock, and other holdings, minus all financial responsibilities).
- *Leasehold improvements.* If you are planning to rent a commercial location or redesign a room within your home strictly for business, estimate cleaning and restoration costs in this statement.

By investing the time and energy into this portion of the business plan, you will absorb the numbers into your consciousness and be able to recognize, at a glance, when your costs exceed your profit margin or when you are in a position to start expanding.

If money matters are absolutely beyond your comprehension at this point, it would pay to hire someone to work along with you in developing the financial pages of the plan. There are business consultants and accountants who will probably charge you a substantial amount, or you can approach the accounting or business department of the nearest college and see if there is a qualified student available to help you.

No matter whom you find to assist you, however, be sure that you stay involved in the process ... the discipline and hard work will guarantee success. ■

Notes

Key Points

_____

_____

_____

_____

Personal Thoughts

_____

_____

_____

_____

_____

_____

Additional Research

_____

_____

_____

_____

_____

14

Financing Your Business

Starting your business without having sufficient capital is setting yourself up for problems from the beginning. Under-capitalization is cited as one of the major reasons why businesses do not succeed; however, this simply boils down to bad planning.

If you research and record all the goals, marketing data, equipment and supply requirements, and financial needs of your venture before actually opening the doors, you will be able to see at a glance how much you need to get going, and *why you need it*. That way, there will be no surprises and no reason that your business should suffer from lack of capitalization.

It is important to have the financial resources to cover all your preliminary planning and start-up costs, including expenses incurred to research the feasibility of your business and expenses required to set up shop, from equipment and supplies to advertising and utility set-up charges, in addition to a surplus to carry you over personally until the business becomes productive. The Cash Flow Statement and Projected Expense Charts provided in Chapter 8 will help you determine these expenses.

If, after drawing up your business plan (Chapter 13), you find that your personal resources are not enough to open the business, there are other options available.

The four most common methods include starting the business on a part-time basis while holding a full-time job to cover expenses, taking on a limited partner, going to friends or family members for the money you need, or applying for a loan through a commercial lender or the Small Business Administration (SBA). There are, of course, pros and cons to each of these options.

Moonlighting

Starting your business on a part-time or "moonlighting" basis is a decision that must be made based on the nature of the business. If you are planning to capitalize on your skills in upholstering, for example, you should have no trouble building up the business at night and on weekends.

It is perfectly feasible to start small, using your garage or a spare room as your production facility and purchasing an answering machine for potential customers to leave a message while you are at your regular job. When you get home, you simply call them back to discuss prices and arrange a time when it is convenient to pick up the piece of furniture to be upholstered.

On the other hand, if you are planning to start a temporary help agency, for example, it would be in your best interest to go into it on a full-time, dedicated basis, as your potential customers are going to want fast results and will call someone else if they are even slightly discouraged, such as getting a recorded message when they call.

Moonlighting will work with some businesses, but before exploring it as an option you must figure out if your limited availability will affect your credibility, if you really have the time and energy to work at a regular job and try to build a business (not to mention family responsibilities) and whether your ultimate goal is to be self-employed or just to earn a few extra dollars to supplement your base income.

Taking on a Partner

A limited partner is one who will put up the money you need and step into the background to let you run the business the way you see fit. You must be sure, however, to have your lawyer draw up a precise partnership agreement that covers every eventuality. Partnerships are typically entered into with the best intentions and the unwavering belief that the business will be successful.

Since this is not always the case—and even if it were—it is a businesslike move to ensure that such aspects as decision making, distribution of profits and losses, contributions of partners, and handling disputes and changes are outlined and approved by all the partners.

Money brings some happiness.
But, after a certain point,
it just brings more money.

Neil Simon

"Friendly" Financing

The third option, raising capital through friends or family members, is probably one of the most often exercised methods. The advantage of getting a loan from a personal contact is that they know you, undoubtedly trust your ability to make the business go and won't require much in the way of substantiating paperwork, such as complex loan applications, financial statements, etc. In addition, you will most likely be able to negotiate a low interest rate on the loan.

The major disadvantage, according to entrepreneurs who have taken this route, is that the friendly lender may want to provide input on the care and maintenance of your business. This problem, however, can be eliminated by a "cards-on-the-table" discussion prior to accepting the loan. In other words, choose your investor carefully!

The second problem has to do with repayment of the loan. Even though you have a loose agreement in writing with your lender, because of friendship or family ties there may come a point when Uncle Bill needs that $10,000 *tomorrow* to take care of a personal obligation. You can't possibly come up with the money overnight, Uncle Bill gets angry and that whole side of the family turns against you.

On the other hand, your business could fail and you would then be unable to pay Uncle Bill or your old college pal the $5,000 she put up. These are unpleasant situations, so you must be sure in the beginning to think about the importance of the relationship you have with the potential lender, how the best and the worst of situations would affect the situation and whether you then could justify asking for money.

Commercial Lenders

If you are not able to, or decide against approaching friends or relatives for financial assistance, the next step is a bank, a Savings & Loan or a credit union. Before approaching any of these commercial lenders you must have carefully developed your business plan, which will include the following documents:

1. A resumé or statement outlining your background and capability to operate the business, plus a similar statement about any key employees or partners in the business.
2. A statement of business and personal goals.
3. A description of the business, including research of the market for your product or service.
4. Details on how the business is going to be structured (sole proprietorship, partnership, corporation, non-profit status).

5. A projection of profit and loss for a minimum of one year, which forces you to do your homework and investigate how similar businesses in similar locations are doing.

6. An outline of how much money you need—and why—to keep the business solvent and to support yourself and your family for at least a year.

In addition, you will be required to provide a personal balance sheet which lists your assets, such as property, a car, etc., and liabilities like your mortgage payments, credit card debts, etc., and a credit application which outlines your personal financial history (so the lender can make a determination on your ability to pay back the loan). The lender will follow through by requesting a credit report from an independent agency, such as TRW, to help them make their decision.

The main thing to remember when applying for a loan with a commerical institution is that lenders aren't as concerned about how much money they loan as they are about how and when they are going to get the money back!

Presenting Your Case

Once you have your business plan and other paperwork prepared, decide which lending association you want to approach. Certainly, if you have a stable record with a checking or savings account at your regular bank or S&L, that is the place to try first. Set up an appointment with the bank manager or loan officer to make your request and explain why you feel your business venture is worth their investment.

Be aware, however, that banks are more likely to provide you with a loan payable within five or ten years, as opposed to Savings & Loans, which are more interested in long-term loans, such as for mortgages. Credit unions operate in a manner similar to banks. However, you generally have to be a member.

If you do belong to a credit union, it could be your best bet, as they offer lower interest rates, and can be more flexible in their determinations.

If, for some reason, you do not want to run a loan through your bank, consider talking with other local small business owners. Very often, they can steer you to a regional, often independently owned bank or S&L which is sympathetic to and supportive of new businesses. In that case, proceed as mentioned above and arrange a meeting with the manager or loan officer.

Paying Back the Loan

When you apply for financing, whether through a friend, relatives, lending institution, a venture capitalist, or under any other type of arrangement, the burden of proof as it relates to repayment rests with you.

No one would knowingly grant a loan to an individual or a business that they had doubts about. As a borrower, your responsibility is to show that you will be able to pay back the loan according to the terms agreed to by you and the lender. This can be done through a credit history that indicates you have a sense of responsibility.

Present your case in a friendly yet professional manner. Be realistic and honest about your needs. Do not underbid because of fear that you will not get a loan if you ask for too much. It is always better to start with a higher figure than you actually need so you have a strong negotiating edge.

In addition, most lenders have a pretty good idea about start-up and operating costs of new businesses and are much less likely to give you, and risk losing, a small loan for a business they know calls for more capital. They will be more willing to work with you if you are realistic and obviously knowledgeable about your needs.

If, after your first try, the answer is no, ask for reasons why you are being turned down so you can restructure your presention. Turn opposition into a learning tool to redefine and polish your material and to develop new negotiating strategies. There are always other potential lenders you can approach, and the law of averages dictates that you will get your loan if the idea is solid and it is apparent that you have researched the feasibility of starting a business in your particular area.

The Small Business Administration

The Small Business Administration (SBA) often goes where no other lender will tread and, as such, is a lender of last resort. It is a government agency that is well known for providing financing to entrepreneurs who have been repeatedly turned down by commercial lenders, which in fact, you generally must do before the SBA will consider backing you.

After your loan request with a commercial institution has been denied, you can file an application with the nearest branch of the SBA. It is a good idea to make an appointment with a Service Corps of Retired Executives (SCORE) representative, who volunteers his or her time to the SBA-SCORE program to advise new and established business owners. Your SCORE representative will be able to lead you through the complex paperwork required by the SBA before they make a decision.

In addition, the SCORE volunteers are usually straightforward, knowledgeable men and women who will walk through your business plans with you and offer constructive suggestions. Once the paperwork is completed, a commercial lender will make the loan under the SBA Lender Certification Program, knowing that the government is willing to insure it.

We recommend this option only after you have been turned down by three or more banks, because of the time involved in gaining approval and also because of the extensive follow-up reports required by the SBA. It is, however, a viable option and one that has helped thousands of dedicated entrepreneurs realize their goals.

Venture Capitalists

Money is available to businesses that are already established and seeking working or expansion capital from groups of investors known as *venture capitalists*. These groups can vary from a few local businessmen with money to invest, to major investment companies connected with large corporations or financial organizations.

Venture capital is not like a straightforward business loan. It is usually dependent on a minimum $100,000 investment and, therefore, is not suited to every business situation. Typically, venture capitalists are interested in companies that have a track record, a proven position in the market and a solid growth projection.

But, like a bank or other lending association, venture capitalists want to see a written business plan and a prospectus of future projections. They are looking at your background, the market, the kind of funding you want and your past financial record. Since venture capitalists are looking to earn from ten to fifteen percent on their investment over a relatively short period, they will want to spend a great deal of time talking with you and your associates, customers and suppliers.

Before considering venture capital, we advise discussing it carefully with an attorney who can help you investigate different groups to figure out the best investment structure, and who can work with their attorney on drawing up an agreement that protects you. Many venture capitalists will want to own part of your company.

This is an option to be considered only when your company is well-established and undergoing rapid growth pains and should be approached with great understanding of the situation.

Other Options for Financing

Loan companies, such as Household Finance and Beneficial Finance, are a source of funding. However, interest rates are high and they will generally want to have substantial collateral, such as the equity in your house, on record before making a loan.

Insurance companies. Your insurance carrier may be willing to make an investment in your small business, using your insurance policy as collateral. Or, you may even have enough cash value in your policy, depending on the face amount, to provide substantial start-up capital. If this is the case, you will only be required to pay quarterly or semi-annual interest payments on the cash value you have taken out.

In this instance, a factoring company 'buys' your accounts receivables and advances you a percentage of the full amount due. This is a viable option for well-established service companies that work on a billing basis.

Co-signer. If you have a relative or friend who is already an established business owner or, at least, a home-owner with a solid credit rating, it might be worth your while to ask if they would co-sign on a loan application with you. Although you are still responsible for repayment of the loan, the bank is assured that, in the event you default for any reason, the co-signer will guarantee the obligation. It is often difficult to find someone who will do this, but again it doesn't hurt to ask, especially if it is a last resort.

Starting Small

Even if you know your particular business is valid and that you have the ability to make it succeed, be certain that your business plan is realistic. If you have chosen to start a business on a grand scale but have minimal capital and little business experience, it may be best to begin a smaller, less elaborate operation at first.

You'll require less "seed money" and put yourself in a low-risk position while learning the ropes and seeing if you can handle all the variables of business ownership while making it grow.

Smaller businesses have proven to be a great way to learn the successful methods, as well as a vehicle for ironing out the many small details that are often overlooked until you actually start taking care of day-to-day situations.

The profits you gain from a smaller venture can be used to expand or invest in bigger business ideas. And, an added bonus is that when you are ready to approach investors or lending institutions, you will be able to show them that you already have a solid track record and a working knowledge of business procedures.

---

*The journey of a thousand miles
begins with a single step.*

Chinese Proverb

What To Do When Asking for Money

Be sure to ask. This may seem like a gross statement of the obvious, but you would be amazed at the number of small business owners we talk to who never ask because they are afraid of being turned down.

Unless you are independently wealthy and pursuing your business as a humanitarian effort, it is unlikely that you are in a position to run your business and earn enough money to support you, your family and the operation—especially during the first year. Remember the old adage: It takes money to make money.

If you run a low-budget business you will probably get a low-budget response. If you are determined to make it work, be sure you have sufficient capital to make it work the right way. Fear *is* often a factor: "I don't want to ask, in case they say no." Well, that's the worst thing that can happen. But, if you persevere and are serious about your venture, someone will inevitably say yes!

And don't overlook friends and family; they can be your most ardent cheerleaders and supporters if you have given them reason in the past to believe you are responsible and determined to succeed.

Know how much you need. Lenders are familiar with the financial demands of business operation and will respect your request if you have obviously done your homework and can talk sensibly about your needs.

Be direct and confident. If you believe in your business and in your ability to make it work, others will be convinced. Never apologize for mistakes you feel you have made in the past and do not present the pathetic picture of someone who could make everything work if they just had enough money.

Simply present the facts honestly, even if it includes revealing an error in judgment you have made somewhere along the line, and assure the lender that they will be making a smart decision by investing in you.

Think positively. If you need $50,000, ask for $50,000. Never underestimate the potential to provide. Even if you are approaching family members, you may be surprised to find that dear Cousin Fred has a $250,000 nest egg socked away. Anyway, it is easier to negotiate and deal with one lender for a single amount than it is to keep paperwork and relationships strong with several, all of whom have contributed a little to the pot.

Ask again. If they trusted you once and you have lived up to the stipulations of the contract, ask again. That goes for commercial lending institutions as well as friends and relatives. A proven record is what it's all about and if you have established yours, keep it active.

Know when to borrow. If you have worked out your business plan and know you can survive while getting the business off the ground, start exploring your financing options ahead of time. Don't wait until the fifth month rolls around, when you will be forced to act frantically and could put you in the position of accept a less-than-favorable situation. The same theory applies if your business is already established. By examining your financial position on a regular basis, you will be able to project how much you will need at a given point for expansion purposes. Be prepared.

Don't borrow if it is not necessary. Many business can be started for under $500. This is called "starting on a shoestring" and can be done with a variety of businesses. Services, for example, often rely strictly on the owner's knowledge and expertise and can be set up quickly and inexpensively.

If this is the case with the business you have in mind, then try to avoid borrowing capital. It can be an expensive and timely proposition. In addition, if, after a projected period of time, the business is showing the kind of profit you can work with while growing, then the smart decision is to utilize the funds and put them back into the operation.

Establishing Credit

Is it possible to get a loan even if you have never established credit? Yes, it is. Many people still prefer to pay cash, rather than incur high interest charges on loans or credit cards. They can still qualify for a loan based on personal assets or by having a friend or relative with a good credit rating who is willing to co-sign. This puts the obligation on the co-signer, so be sure the terms of the loan are clearly spelled out in a written agreement to the satisfaction of everyone involved in the transaction.

However, if your personal assets are minimal and you cannot find a co-signer, the best bet is to put off starting the business for four to six months while you establish credit.

The best place to start is with a major department store such as Sears or J.C. Penney. They issue credit cards based on a very simple examination of your income and employment history. Charge about $100 worth of merchandise when you receive the card and pay it off according to the schedule provided. Within a few months, you will have proven yourself to be credit worthy, which will greatly improve your chances of getting a loan from a lending institution.

Another way to establish credit—and credibility—is to open a checking account at the bank you have decided to approach for a loan. They generally require a minimum deposit of between $50 and $100. Make it a point to meet the branch manager and/or the loan officer and to establish an on-going relationship with them by stopping by to say hello when you are in the bank.

Within a few months, apply for a small personal loan, working with your new acquaintance, of course. Make your payments according to the prearranged schedule. Then when you are ready to request a more substantial amount of money to cover your start-up expenses, you will be recognized as a customer with a loan history at that institution. ■

15

Record Keeping:
Your Business Lifeline

The motivating factor in any business is profit, which can be defined as the money left over after all the bills, for everything from supplies to rent and salaries to taxes, are paid.

Building a profitable business is not something that can be left to chance; it must be planned and a systematic method of record keeping must be developed to help you control income and expenses.

You should expect that during the early days of your business, your profits are going to be minimal as you become established. But it is possible, with even simple record keeping procedures, to prepare yourself for lean periods and control day-to-day expenses to ensure that you are, at least, breaking even. In addition, financial records are required for tax purposes and dealing with them systematically can eliminate an incredibly overwhelming task at tax time.

Record Keeping Can Be Simple

Some people cringe at the thought of record keeping or feel it is a waste of valuable time. Usually, these attitudes are based on a lack of knowledge and the feeling that it is an overwhelming task. There is, however, no other way to analyze your cash flow and make sure you are pricing products or services high enough to realize a profit.

In actuality, record keeping is not such a complicated process. If you have ever balanced a checkbook or planned a household budget, you were basically doing several of the same steps that are necessary for implementing a bookkeeping system for your business. And the good news is that keeping your records does not have to be either complicated or time consuming.

We know of entrepreneurs who opt for total simplicity by using the "shoebox" method—every sales record, receipt for expenses and bank statement gets tossed into a box. This system has two distinct drawbacks. One may not become apparent until tax time, when you attempt to wade through the paper to prepare your tax return. (If you hire an accountant to do your taxes, it shouldn't come as a surprise if an additional "combat fee" has been added to the bill.)

The other, more critical drawback is that it is virtually impossible to maintain an accurate picture of your financial situation when you stockpile, rather than record, business transactions. In order to understand your cash flow, it is important to be able to see what monies have come in, what you have paid out, current balances and outstanding debts.

In fact, you should be able to answer the following questions with just a quick review of your records:

- What was my income last year (or week, or month)?
- What were my expenses?
- How do income and expenses compare with last year (or week, or month)?
- What was my profit (or loss) last year (or week, or month)?
- Where can I cut back on expenses?
- Who and how much do I currently owe on outstanding debts?
- Who owes me money and how much?
- What are my assets, liabilities and net worth?
- Is my inventory in line with demand?
- How much cash do I have available? How much credit?

- Am I able to pay myself this month (week)?
- Are my figures in line with projected financial goals?

The primary documents you need, to be able to answer most of these questions, are your Cash Journal, a Balance Sheet, and a Bank Reconciliation. A simple single-entry system, as indicated on the following pages, in which to record disbursements (cash paid out) and receipts (cash taken in) forms the base of your record keeping.

The Double-Entry System

Your accountant will probably utilize a double-entry system, which involves recording each transaction twice; once as a debit (simply the left column of the ledger) and once as a credit (the right column of the ledger). For example, if you were to sell a product for $100, the transactions recorded in a double-entry system would be as follows:

The $100 would be written as a *credit* in your Sales account, since merchandise is going out of the business and $100 would be recorded as a *debit* in your Cash account since money was coming into the business (see page 145).

If you can organize your kitchen,
you can organize your life.

Dr. Louis Parrish

This is a complex and time-consuming process that is often best left to an accountant, as he or she will need the information to create a monthly Trial Balance and other financial statements, including your year-end tax reports.

Single-Entry Bookkeeping

You can, however, have your accountant's office set up a simple single-entry system for you which will tie-in directly with their requirements. Or, check out the standardized book-keeping systems, which provide all the necessary forms and documents in a bound book, stocked by stationery stores.

One of the most widely accepted, ready-made systems is the *Dome Simplified Monthly Bookkeeping Record*. It contains forms for recording monthly income and expenses, summary sheets from which you can create a Balance Sheet and listings of legal deductions for income tax reporting. Instructions are included.

In addition, the trade association for your field should be able to provide you with systems developed exclusively for use in the industry, which you can use 'as-is' or adapt according to specific circumstances within your business.

The final method is to purchase a Cash Journal book and set up your own monthly system. A typical example is outlined later in this chapter for *Office Assistance*, a small typing service which has been operating for one month. Any of the above mentioned methods are acceptable, as long as you understand the entry process and can "read" the results.

Make Record Keeping a Daily Task

The easiest way (short of paying someone else to do it) to be sure your records are kept up-to-date is to incorporate the task into your daily or weekly routine. Many small business owners make it a habit to enter their sales, expenses and other financial information at the end of each working day. It keeps them continually aware of their financial situation and ensures that there will never be any cash-flow surprises.

The process probably takes no more than 15 minutes for normal transactions, but will save hours of pencil-pushing and frustration down the line. And, more important, you'll know where you stand financially.

Debit & Credit in Bookkeeping

Debits include:	*Credits include:*
• Cash receipts	• Cash payments
• Purchases	• Sales of services or merchandise
• Expenses, such as rent and wages	• Earnings, including interest earned

---

Setting Up the Books

Using Office Assistance, a secretarial service, as an example, we can examine the various elements required for basic record-keeping duties.

Bill Miller, president of Office Assistance, has been in business for one month. Two months ago, he opened a new business bank account with $10,000, his start-up capital from a personal savings account.

At the same time, he rented a small office in a downtown building for $350 a month, but had to pay the first month's rent and a deposit of the last month's rent, for a total outlay of $700.

His fictitious name statement, which he got approved through the local County Clerk's office, ran $10, and publishing it in a regional newspaper was $45.

The initial month's lease and a deposit on a state-of-the-art typewriter cost him $275, plus $50 for a maintenance agreement. However, he will own the $2,000 typewriter when his payment schedule is completed.

He found a brand new calculator at a garage sale for $25 and is going to use a desk, table, lamp and chairs brought from home (value $350) to decorate the office. Phone installation was $150, but he purchased a two-line telephone for $79.50.

An artist friend designed his logo and letterhead on a computer for only $25 and a $6.95 lunch. He had his stationery ($35), business cards ($60), and brochures ($23.50) produced through a local copy shop for a total of $118.50.

Since he doesn't know how to type, Bill hired his niece to work 20 hours a week for $5 per hour on an independent contractor basis so he doesn't have to pay social security or unemployment taxes.

A 2 x 2-inch display ad in the local newspaper cost him $370 for a week, so he is planning to mail 100 of his brochures to local businesses selected from the phone book. Stamps: $25 for the mailing. Office supplies, including typing paper, staples, paper clips, etc., set him back $45. A journal for record keeping cost $7.95.

He purchased a packet of invoices for $5.95 and, during the first month, has billed and been paid $700. However, he has two accounts who still owe him a total of $400. Bill dutifully records information in his cash journal at the end of each working day. He uses source documents, including his check book register, receipts from cash purchases and billing invoices as the basis for his entries. The two pages following are for May (prior to opening the doors of his business) and June (his first actual month in business).

Bill's expenses for May and June were $2704.75. Of course, part of that is for start-up expenses, such as deposits on his rent and typewriter, installation costs, and one-time fictitious name filing and publishing. His income for the first month was $700. By deducting his expenses from his income, he can see that, at the moment, his business is showing a loss of $2,004.75.

Although Bill has only been in business for a month, he is curious about his company's financial worth and decides to

Office Assistance
Cash Journal for May

Date	Check # Invoice #	Detail	(Debit) Expense	(Credit) Income
5/1	100	Rawlins Real Estate (Rent & dep)	$ 700.00	
5/5	101	County Clerk (Fictitious Name)	10.00	
5/7	102	The Herald (publishing FNS)	45.00	
5/9	103	Ed's Keyboards (IBM 1-mo. & dep)	275.00	
5/9	104	Ed's Keyboards (Maint. agreement)	50.00	
5/12	105	Mary Smith (Calculator purchase)	25.00	
5/18	106	Telephone company (line installation)	150.00	
5/20	107	Phone Store (2-line phone)	79.50	
5/22	108	Ray Brown (logo design)	25.00	
5/24	Cash	The Hungry Dog (lunch/Ray Brown)	6.95	
5/28	109	The Copy Spot (brochures, cards, etc.)	118.50	
5/29	110	The Herald (advertising)	370.00	
		Total Income & Expense (May)	$1,854.95	$00.00

Office Assistance
Cash Journal for June

Date	Check # Invoice #	Detail	(Debit) Expense	(Credit) Income
6/4	111	U.S.P.O (Stamps for mailing)	$ 25.00	
6/6	112	Office Stationers		
		(supplies, invoices, etc.)	58.90	
6/7	A1	W. Smith		$ 62.50
6/8	A2	Art Association		112.50
6/9	A3	T. Williams		22.00
6/9	113	Judy Miller (typing fee)	100.00	
6/10	A4	Bank of Cutterville		75.00
6/10	A5	WKTR-FM		120.50
6/13	A6	J. Johnson		43.50
6/15	114	Rawlins Real Estate (rent)	350.00	
6/15	A7	C. Lewis		73.50
6/15	A8	R. Swell		90.00
6/16	115	Judy Miller (typing fee)	100.00	
6/19	A9	W. Smith		52.50
6/23	116	Judy Miller (typing fee)	100.00	
6/26	117	Phone company (bill)	15.90	
6/27	A10	K. Black		48.00
6/30	118	Judy Miller (salary)	100.00	
		Total Income & Expense (June)	$849.80	$700.00

work up a balance sheet to get the answer. The calculation, as indicated in the following example, is the amount owned (assets) minus the amount due to creditors (liabilities) which equals his worth.

Balance Sheet as of June 30

Assets		Liabilities	
Cash on hand & in bank	$ 7,995.25	Ed's Keyboards	$ 1,725.00
(Capital balance & June Income)		*(Balance on IBM)*	
		Unpaid rent *(July)*	350.00
Office Equipment	2,104.50	Taxes *(estimated)*	75.00
(includes full value of IBM even though not paid off)			
Office Furniture	350.00	**Liabilities**	$ 2,150.00
Accounts Receivable			
(outstanding invoices for work already done)	400.00		
Total Assets	$10,745.25	***CAPITAL**	$ 8,595.25
		Total Liabilities	$10,745.25

The figure Bill is most interested in is the *CAPITAL amount in the Liabilities column. This is the amount remaining after what Bill owes is subtracted from his current assets and is what his business is worth at the end of June. In other words, if he decided to try and sell his business right now, he could realistically ask that amount as a sale price. Of course, Bill probably wouldn't get that amount because he has not yet become established enough to warrant someone buying the business, unless they were looking for a "turnkey" operation— in other words, a business they could just walk into and get going immediately.

This information is valuable when Bill goes to apply for expansion capital or for credit on future purchases he plans to make, i.e., a photocopier, a computer and new furniture. His balance sheet will change each time he prepares it (probably quarterly in the future) as business increases, bringing in more income and reducing his debts.

In the meantime, the Balance Sheet gives Bill a tool to use when comparing the financial standing of his business this month against future months and years. It also keeps him current on what he owns, to whom he owes money, and his major sources of income.

The same procedure is used in developing a personal balance sheet, which possibly would be needed to establish credibility when applying for a loan. Assets would include furniture, automobiles, jewelry, your home and other tangibles, while liabilities would consist of outstanding loans and other major debts.

Bank Statement Reconciliation

Another important step that Bill must handle monthly is reconciling his bank statement against his checkbook register. He simply marks off the checks in his register that have cleared per the statement and the deposits which have been credited, and deducts any service charges for the previous month from his balance.

Bill then adds up all the outstanding checks—those listed in his register which have not cleared by the closing date indicated on the bank statement—and *deducts* them from the balance indicated on his bank statement. He adds up any deposits which have not yet been credited to his account and then *adds* them to the balance, as indicated below.

Balance per bank statement	$ 7,953.44
Plus: Deposits not credited	+325.00
Minus: Outstanding checks	−115.90
New Balance	$ 8,162.54

The new balance figure should match that listed in his checkbook register and, in this case, it does. If, however, the statement and the register did not reconcile, Bill would have a customer representative at the bank review his statement and banking activity for the past month.

A Simplified System for Charting Calls and Orders

It's absolutely crucial that you keep good records. How you accomplish this can range from the very basic to using an accountant if the size of your business dictates it. Because you're most likely starting small and at home, we'll focus on the basic methods.

A simple record keeping system will allow you to track all the information you need on a few simple charts. Take a three-ring binder and fill it with copies of the following record keeping sheets. (Have them enlarged at a copy shop.) These are the basics you need:

- Sales Call Report Sheet,
- Order Form,
- Lead (Prospect) Form, and
- Daily/Weekly Summary.

As your business grows you'll need to adjust your record-keeping system accordingly, and there may come a point where the simple methods described above no longer work for you. As the need arises, do some research at the local library about basic accounting methods. Remember: *The most important thing is that you keep records that are clear to you, and that you substantiate expenses for income tax purposes.* ■

Sales Call Report Sheet

Date	Time	Talked To	Result	N/A*	WrN*	DIS*	NNL*	B*	Send Info	Call Back

N/A - No Answer
DIS - Disconnected
B - Busy (Try Back)

WrN - Wrong Number
NNL - No New Listing
Rep _____

Telemarketing Order Form

Sold To
Name_____

Address_____

City_____State____Zip_____

Telephone (Day) _____(Evening) _____

Ship To
Name_____

Address _____

City_____State____Zip_____

Telephone (Day) _____ (Evening)_____

Order Number_____

Payment Method   Check No. _____Bank_____

Credit Card ___ MC ___ VISA ___ Discover ___ AMEX

Card # _____ Exp. Date _____ BIN _____

Item #	Description	Quantity	Unit Price	Total

Comments:	Subtotal	
	Taxes	
	Shipping	
	TOTAL	

Shipping Info:_____

Sold by_____ Date_____

Lead (Prospect) Form

Date _____

Client (Project) Name _____

Name of Prospect_____
Company (If Applicable) _____
Address_____
City _____ State _____ Zip _____
Work Phone _____ Home Phone _____

Rating: Hot Lead _____ Warm_____ Lukewarm_____
___Knows Product/Service   ___Unaware of Product/Service
___Has Used Before   ___Unfavorable Response
___Send Info   ___Ready to make decision
___Needs More Time   ___Do Not Call Back
___Give lead to:
 Best time to call _____ Comments_____

Lead (Prospect) Form

Date _____

Client (Project) Name_____

Name of Prospect _____
Company (If Applicable) _____
Address_____
City _____ State _____Zip_____
Work Phone _____ Home Phone _____

Rating: Hot Lead _____ Warm_____ Lukewarm _____
___Knows Product/Service   ___Unaware of Product/Service
___Has Used Before   ___Unfavorable Response
___Send Info   ___Ready to make decision
___Needs More Time   ___Do Not Call Back
___Give lead to:
 Best time to call _____ Comments _____

Daily Summary

Week Ending_____ Project _____
Representative _____
Shift _____
Total hours worked_____

Date _____

Total Leads	Leads Used	Sales	No Interest	Call Backs	Send Info	No Ans.	Wrong Number	NNL	Misc.

Comments

Weekly Summary

Project _____
Representative _____
Shift _____
Total shifts worked_____Total hours worked_____

Week Ending _____

Total Leads	Leads Used	Sales	No Interest	Call Backs	Send Info	No Ans.	Wrong Number	NNL	Misc.

Comments

16

Pricing for Profits

One of the toughest problems that small-business owners face is establishing prices that, on one hand, the market will bear while, on the other, will cover overhead and guarantee a profit.

Often new business owners price their product unrealistically low in order to get sales, but this is not an advisable practice. Realistic pricing indicates your confidence in what you are selling and if you value your service, so will the customer.

Today's consumers realize that they can't get something worthwhile for nothing, so don't be afraid to establish prices that will work toward your profit goals.

In telemarketing, rates vary considerably. In general, however, most service bureaus we investigated average between $25 and $50 per calling hour. Some bureaus charge different fees for one-job-only clients than for those on a retainer. They reach this point through a number of different combinations and options, as follows:

1. Flat hourly fees (starting at $20 per hour) based on a 100 hour minimum, *plus* set-up costs of $500 to $2,000 per job to cover the cost of training, script development and customized forms for record keeping.
2. Hourly fees based on actual calling hour (which means approximately 30 minutes of phone time per hour based on allowances for paperwork, wrong numbers, no answers, call-backs, etc.), *plus* training fees set at fifty percent of the hourly rate, *and* a flat fee of $10 to $20 for script development and administration of the account.

3. A basic telephone line reimbursement, *plus* a percentage of actual sales, *and* a weekly retainer.

Some clients will want to try a test of your service before making a commitment for long-term telemarketing. In this situation, it is perfectly feasible to establish a "Test Rate" based on a minimum number of hours and involving a normal crew.

Variances on Inbound Calls

The pricing variables given above are primarily for outgoing calls. However, on incoming telemarketing, which may involve order taking or customer service, similar structures are developed with the main exception being a package that includes a "per incoming call" rate over and above a retainer or flat hourly fee.

In addition, you will definitely want to charge extra for any additional service you provide your clients, including label making, mailing, xeroxing and follow-up calls. If you plan to do any consulting, be aware that the national average rate is $125 per hour with variances ranging from $50 to $300, depending on your location and reputation.

When setting prices, you must take into consideration the cost of labor and materials (supplies), overhead, and profit. Labor costs will include wages and benefits to your employees. Most telemarketing-service bureau owners try to make a net profit of from fifteen to twenty-five percent, although this figure, too, can vary. Others use the simple labor-to-fee ratio to determine fees; estimating their labor costs and doubling the figure to arrive at a base fee.

No matter which pricing structure you choose—one of those outlined above or a unique system which encompasses aspects of each—be sure to discuss it with your accountant before putting your rates down on paper. It may even be necessary to tailor your pricing to individual jobs, based on the specifics that each client needs or wants.

If Clients Don't Pay

Be firm about your payment schedule from the time of your first meeting and the majority (ninety-five percent according to most telemarketing service owners) of clients will pay the balance according to your expectations. This is especially true if you make it a practice to request a deposit on service and payment on a weekly basis. Most clients are going to be extremely prompt about payment since all you have to do to encourage them is to stop all activity on their particular telemarketing project.

If, however, you run into a slow-paying customer or a person who offers the flimsy excuse that they are withholding payment because they were dissatisfied with the service you provided, you have several avenues of recourse.

The first step is to send a personal letter reminding the client of the amount due and requesting payment within a reasonable period of time (ten days is considered reasonable). State that you realize they may have forgotten about the bill, even if you know they haven't. In other words, give them the benefit of the doubt. In most cases, this will result in immediate payment.

Next, try calling the client or make a personal visit to their office. Explain that you have provided services in good faith and have expenses which are covered by your getting paid. If this doesn't elicit a check or promise of payment in the near future, explain that you will be forced to take further action. If they ask what you intend to do, just say that they will be hearing from you or your representative within a few days, which gives you a chance to figure out what the next step will be.

One thing you can do is to ask your lawyer to send a standard collection letter on his or her letterhead. Often this tactic will be just the fuel needed to spark them into writing a check. It will cost you—probably your attorney's hourly charge—but is worth it if the bill is substantial.

Small claims court is another option. Although it takes time, it is inexpensive. The main drawback is that claims are limited to debts up to a certain amount (anywhere from $1,200 to $2,000 depending on your state).

There are two things to keep in mind when taking someone to small claims court. One: judgment may not be made in your favor depending on the way the judge weighs both sides of the story, which means you lose the amount due as well as the time and money invested in filing the claim. Two: even if a judgement is made in your favor, it doesn't guarantee that you will receive payment immediately if the client still decides to hold back, or claims to be under financial duress.

Collection agencies take a percentage, and it can be a large one, of the final amount collected as payment. Basically they hound the client and send nasty letters indicating how their credit rating is going to be affected by not paying your bill. Sometimes it works and sometimes it doesn't. ■

Sample Contract
Telemark Incorporated
1 Main Street
555-5555
Contract for Telemarketing Services

Contact Name _____

Name of Organization _____

Address _____

Phone _____ Secondary Contact _____

Primary Product _____

Type of Service Required _____

Date to Begin _____ Pricing Schedule _____

Set-Up Charge _____ Billing Method _____

Deposit Amount _____ Date Received _____

Names of Reps on Job _____

_____

_____

_____

Expected Results _____

_____

_____

_____

Extra Services _____

_____

_____

Signed By _____

Title _____ Date _____

*If cancellation is made one week prior to the start date indicated above, 50% of the deposit will be returned. TELEMARK Incorporated retains the right to keep 100% of the deposit if cancellation is made after that time, except in the case of extreme emergencies, in which case, 50% of deposit amount will be returned. Initial _____

17

The Logic of Telemarketing

The motivating factors of many of the telemarketers we interviewed include the following:

Low Start-up Costs. There are successful telemarketing services that have been started with very little capital. Since the focus is on a service that does not require a fancy retail location, and because you probably have telephone equipment already installed in your home, it is feasible to get started for under $500 in a single-line, outcalling owner-operated business.

The greater the difficulty, the more glory there is in surmounting it. Skillful pilots gain their reputation from storms and tempests.

Anonymous

A perfect example of this type of start-up is illustrated by the experience of Tim Landsdown of Los Angeles. Four years ago, he took a temporary job in telephone sales for a cable television station. Realizing the potential in the business, he set up a corner of his living room with a desk, comfortable chair and a telephone extension connected to a headset.

After approaching 20 companies, he secured his first account: a jewelry manufacturer who desperately wanted to make contact with the thousands of jewelry shops and gift shops nationwide. This company had the inventory and the money to invest in marketing, but not the know-how—and that's where Tim came in. Within the first two weeks, he had made personal contact with and developed a mailing list of 500 qualified buyers. As an additional service, Tim offered to handle the folding, envelope stuffing, stamping, bulk-mail sorting and mailing of price lists and brochures for 4 cents a piece.

Tim made a net profit of $375 his first week in business. Last year, his full-service telemarketing company grossed $225,000, boasted a full-time staff of ten telemarketers, who work two shifts handling three to five major accounts per month! Tim claims that he has been able to "grow into" the business, both financially and professionally, very smoothly.

High Profit Potential.   Despite its low-risk appeal, it is possible to earn tremendous money if you promote your service and pay attention to your budget. Service bureaus typically bill a client anywhere from $25 to $150 per hour, depending on the the region of the country, the number of telemarketers working the account and the range of services provided. With careful planning and patience while you get established, profits will start to build quickly, often with the first job.

Creativity.   If you have always enjoyed writing, this business gives you the opportunity to work up exciting, guaranteed-sale scripts for your telemarketing clients. In addition to the satisfaction of creating a profitable 'masterpiece,' you will soon develop a reputation that will ensure your position as a winner in this burgeoning industry.

Flexible Hours.   Telemarketing is a good business to start on a part-time basis. The majority of your clients are going to be selling products or services to people who work for a living, which means that the best time to get through to them is in the evening or on weekends, making it feasible for you to work at another job while you get established.

The only problem with working nights and weekends might be family responsibilities, but most telemarketers claim that they have been able to find solutions that ease the burden on loved ones.

Keep This in Mind

Out of every five prospects you speak to, there will be one who will buy anything from anybody, one who wouldn't buy anything from their own mother and three who are fence sitters . . . and that's where your sales ability comes into play.

The fence sitters may be any one of the following client types: The Window Shopper (indecisive), The Know-it-All (annoying), The Talker (avoids the close) or The Pal (usually wants a deal).

Be aware that there are hundreds of client types out there and you will always be prepared to tailor your presentation accordingly.

That's half the fun of telemarketing!

Interaction with People.   All of the telemarketers we interviewed mentioned how much they enjoy the interesting people they talk to on the job. You will come into contact with folks from all walks of life in your conversations.

A Very Bright Future!   The latest wrinkle in this relatively young telemarketing industry is that magazines are getting into the act. Several are offering their advertisers the option of a toll-free 800 access line that allows readers to call for information that augments a print ad! After hearing a 30-second message, they can leave their name or address to receive even further information or can punch a number on a computerized call monitor that connects them with a representative. We are sure to see many more interesting applications in telemarketing as entrepreneurs enter the field.

Management Checklist

The list below provides you with an overview of the most important management aspects you must keep in mind at all times when starting your service and as you build it into a full-scale telemarketing bureau. Using this list as a general guide will help you to maintain control of the overall operation as well as to keep individual assignments moving along smoothly.

1. Outline your client's goals, i.e., expected long-term results, and the time-frame in which they expect to see these results. Start to work up a plan of action for the campaign.
2. Make sure you have enough operating capital to hire telemarketing representatives, upgrade equipment and prepare correlated documentation to handle orders, and control calls. If necessary, request a deposit from your client to cover "set-up" costs.
3. Prepare a campaign analysis, outlining specific information about the product or service you will be promoting, including cost, benefits and even drawbacks, colors available, sizes and other specifications, shipping information, billing details, etc. Create a product/service information sheet, keyed for easy access by reps during a telephone presentation and gather all available support literature including brochures, specification sheets and pricing from your client.
4. Develop an objection file, covering every possible response your reps may get on the telephone plus ways to overcome them. Create an objection sheet, keyed for easy access by reps during a presentation.

*If you want to make money,
go where the money is.*

Joseph P. Kennedy

5. Decide, with your client, how orders are to be handled, including what credit cards, type of check, CODs, and so on will be accepted. Also decide whether there is to be a brochure or information packet that will be mailed to interested parties upon request. Create an order/response information sheet, keyed for easy access by reps during a presentation.
6. Start working on the telephone presentation script. Try it out on your client and, if possible, do a test run with it to see if it can be improved. (Every script *can* be improved.) Rewrite until it works.
7. Develop your record keeping documents for the assignment, such as order forms, survey reports, summaries, call records, etc.
8. Work with your clients in targeting the kind of audience they hope to reach, then review available lists through list brokers, or have a custom list designed that provides the names, addresses, and telephone numbers of the desired market.
9. Develop a training guide based on the product or service and hire your telemarketing crew and any support staff. One good tip we heard is to hire a few backup telephone reps. This covers you in case of burnout, illness or lack of sales ability—all of which typically occur right in the middle of a telemarketing push. Even if you have to put your backups on part-time pay status to keep them active, it can be well worth it if it saves a campaign.

10. If at all possible, conduct a test campaign of between 50 and 100 calls to monitor your telemarketers and evaluate the effectiveness of the script. If more training is needed or modifications are called for on the script, now is the time to do it.

11. Develop evaluation techniques that give you the opportunity to review and analyze your budget, personnel, and response to the campaign, broken down by orders, refusals, requests for more information, no answers, wrong numbers, and any other applicable categories. This, in addition to client feedback, will let you know whether or not you need to make modifications to your service.

After you have handled a couple of telemarketing campaigns, there will be certain aspects of each that you can incorporate into new assignments. For example, you will know that certain call records are easier for your reps to use than others; the optimum one will probably just need a few refinements to fit into the work plan for each new project.

Review of Preliminary Steps

There are some specific things you need to accomplish before you go out there and start your telemarketing business. First, you must have pretty solid idea of the services (inbound, outcalling, mailings, etc.) you'll provide at the start.

Next, you need equipment, as discussed earlier. Finally, you need a method to generate business, meaning advertising and promotion, which we'll get to later. For the moment, however, let's talk about the primary services you plan on providing.

It's probably a safe bet that you've been thinking about your service menu since it was first mentioned a while back. Now is the time to make some decisions, because you can't take another step until that first step is out of the way. If you have not yet decided, have you:

- Gathered some inital "need" data through basic marketing tests?
- Looked into other telemarketing services (for comparative service, price, set-up and information about what the competition's doing)?
- Thought about new ideas or gaps in services currently available?
- Asked a representative group of people (prospective clients) for feedback on your idea(s)?

If you still need to choose your specific service, keep working on it. For the purposes of this book, we'll assume that this decision has been made so we can use the chosen service to illustrate certain points. Let's say, then, that you have chosen to concentrate on outgoing calls to sell consumer products, for the moment anyway, and that you'll expand your service menu down the road.

You've chosen your service, taken care of equipment needs, and done some advertising and promotion . . . now what? No one's beating down your doors for business! What to do?!

Relax. You're going to discover that few telemarketing services—few small businesses, for that matter—get off the ground like a rocket. There's only one reason you should panic if you don't get lots of business right away, and that's if you've made this new telemarketing venture your sole source of projected income. There's a simple way to avoid that problem.

Don't do it . . . unless you are independently wealthy and can cover yourself financially, you should not try to start in this business full time. There are simply too many variables that you cannot control. Better to start part-time, a few jobs here and there, and work your way into the business's growth.

This will not only help you ease your way into the job, but will help you maintain interest and momentum because you won't be facing dashed expectations of immediate success. The best advice we can offer vis-a-vis starting the job and maintaining momentum is:

1. Start slowly.
2. Grow steadily.
3. Maintain a positive attitude.
4. Learn as much as possible.

Getting a Line on Information

The telemarketing business has become highly specialized, and there is specific knowledge you *must* have to stay competitive. Scripting and record-keeping techniques, equipment facts, marketing approaches—you'll need to nurture and build upon all these to succeed in your business.

There are numerous sources from which you can gain this knowledge. Books are invaluable, although there seems to be a shortage of them for the industry. Trade publications offered by direct marketing associations (listed in the Resources chapter) are extremely valuable. Professional seminars, a short-term job with a telemarketing outfit, college classes—all are ways to build on your skills and keep up with your competitors.

One of the most overlooked sources of knowledge for professional growth is the people you are in contact with, both your clients and the leads you are calling. *Ask and listen* to them when they give you feedback about the work you do.

They may not be experts in the field—they may not even know what telemarketing really is—but they do know how they like to be treated and they know what works to sell them on something. And, since you're in the business of trying to convince people to buy a product or your service, it can only help you to listen when they tell you what they do or do not like about your presentation. ■

18

The Telemarketing Script

You definitely need a script in telemarketing, for the following reasons:

1. So you aren't caught off guard by questions or comments,
2. To keep your presentation direct, short and exciting, and
3. To sound authoritative and professional.

It isn't necessary to follow the script word-for-word. In fact, this is generally the case only with inexperienced telemarketers or when very specific controls are being demanded by the client. Usually, the script serves as a guide. Once you know the basic points that are to be covered, you would refer to it only occasionally.

The ten main points to keep in mind when writing your presentation script are provided below. For examples of these points, see the sample script on pages 174–176.

1. Keep the words simple and easily understandable and keep sentences short and to the point. You should be able to cover everything in the way of introductory material in 60 to 90 seconds to ensure that you don't lose your audience.
2. Introduce yourself and clearly outline your reason for calling within the first two sentences. If your call is based on a referral or a return card in response to a mail offer, mention it. Even if you are calling from a telephone directory for a specific city, you might say, "We are giving

residents of Anytown, like you, the opportunity to take advantage of a special offer."

If there is a strong likelihood that the prospective customer has never heard of the company or product, be sure to offer a brief explanation so they aren't forced to guess, or get frustrated and hang up.

3. Establish rapport with the prospect by asking a personal question. It can be as simple as "How are you today?" or topical, "What did you think about those election results?" (Even if they didn't vote, you have made a personal connection.)

If you have called before, you should have made note of the results on your lead sheet and will have an idea of the kind of comment to make. For example, if they couldn't talk to you last time because of a sick child, you should inquire about the child's health. This will give you a great advantage based on familiarity.

4. Make sure that none of the words or phrases within your presentation script can be misinterpreted because they have several different meanings.

An example of this is a situation that frequently occurs with appointment-making for a field sales staff. The telemarketer says to the prospective customer, "*We'll* be by on Saturday at 1 p.m." rather than specifying that a certain representative will actually be coming by for the appointment.

Many field reps have had doors slammed in their face simply because the prospect was under the impression that the telephone rep would be stopping by or a group (*we*) from the company would be over. It may seem like a foolish misunderstanding, but when it means dollars and time, it should be approached seriously. If shipping is going to take ten days, don't say "It will be there in a week or so," because you can count on getting phone calls on the fifth day.

The Progress of a Phone Presentation

- Introduce Yourself
- Establish Rapport
- Determine Prospect's Needs
- Present Details
- Overcome Objections
- Close the Sale
- Verify Customer Information
- Show Appreciation for Order

Three results are possible at the point of closing the sale:

1. The prospect orders the product or service.
2. They give you a definite no and become a "dead" lead.
3. They request more information. In this case, you send a brochure or other literature and, a week or so later, make a second call.

At that point, they will either order, request even more information (don't give up yet, especially if there is a genuine glimmer of interest), or they will give you a definite no!

5. Use the prospective customer's name at least four times during the presentation, once in the very beginning, again as you conclude outlining the benefits of the product or service you are selling, at the point of trying to close the sale and, of course, when you say goodbye to them.
6. Incorporate "yes" questions that keep the prospect involved. For example, don't ask "Is this a bad time to call?"

because, undoubtedly, it is and you may be told so in no uncertain terms. Instead, get their interest, their willingness to commit to listening for a few minutes while, at the same time get them used to saying "yes" by asking, "I would like one minute of your time to tell you how you can make your life more satisfying [make more money, be happier, have healthier children or whatever]. Sound exciting?" While you may still get the occasional grouch who says "no," the odds are pretty good that most people will be interested.

7. Sell the benefits of owning the product or using the service (known in the industry as selling the sizzle and not the steak). Use descriptions and positive stories to illustrate your points, e.g., "Mr. Bill Smith of your town wrote us a letter to say his super-dooper, double-plated gizmo has been giving him top quality service for three years... he has never even read the exclusive 48-month guarantee booklet and figures he has saved $500 over that time!"

    People typically buy something that saves money, makes them more attractive, gives them more time, satisfies their ego, increases their status in the eyes of the world, or generally makes life more comfortable. By asking the right questions and listening to the answers, you can adapt the benefits to each prospect's individual needs.

8. When you write your presentation, do so from the prospective client's point of view, i.e., how it will benefit them rather than why you want them to buy. To ensure that you are not working strictly from a seller's standpoint, test the script out on friends and family and ask for feedback. Do they feel you have *their* best interests in mind, or is the presentation coming off as a forceful demand to write a check or to sign-up?

9. Include closing lines in your script copy. "Shall I sign you up for our special one year subscription rate?" or "This is an excellent time to order. All you have to do is give me a

credit card number and let me confirm your mailing address. Should I start preparing your order?"

You can reiterate any special bonuses that they are entitled to in your closing, such as, "If we set an appointment today, I will have our representative bring your free whatsit with him. So, I can set that up for Wednesday evening or Saturday afternoon. Which would be better for you?"

10. Use the script as a basis for drawing up a list of objections and rebuttals. For example, if one of the benefits you have outlined is "twenty years of service," you can assume that someone is going to come back with "I've never heard of the company." That objection can be countered by offering a list of satisfied customers, mentioning the company's standing in the industry based on trade association figures, or offering to send out a brochure that outlines the history and growth of the firm. Other general objections and positive rebuttals are provided later in this chapter.

Sample: New Prospect Script

(The product, Compuday, is fictitious.)

Introduction. May I speak with *(prospect's name)*, please? Hello, *(prospect's name)*, this is *(rep's name)* with *(company or product)*.

Establish rapport. How about that rain storm last night? I hope you didn't get caught in it!

Present details. The reason I'm calling today *(prospect's name)* is to tell you about a product that is going to revolutionize the way you organize your time for business and personal tasks.

Finding customer need. Tell me *(prospect's name)*, do you currently use a calendar or a daily planner to keep track of appointments, errands and things that must be done?

Benefits in response to answer. *If not:* Then our Compuday Organizer is going to give you more free time than you ever dreamed imaginable because it will eliminate wasted steps.

If so: Then you realize the importance of being organized and are one of a special few who will truly appreciate the time-saving benefits of Compuday.

Details. Compuday fits into a shirt pocket or a purse, and tells you exactly what you were planning to do at any given time. It's like having your own personal assistant, but you don't have to be wealthy! Here, let me give you an example.

Listen. (Play Compuday message into phone receiver.) See! Sounds like a human voice. Well, in fact, it is! It's my voice. You, of course, would program your Compuday by simply recording the time, day, and event—as far ahead as two months. Compuday organizes the information and reminds you at a prescheduled time. And only your voice can activate it!

Overcoming objections. I can understand your concerns about service, *(prospect's name)*, but let me assure you that if anything were to go wrong, I'm as close as your telephone. However, Compuday comes with a full one-year warranty.

Close. If you order today, I'll include a free leather carrying case. So, shall I write that order up and have it billed to your credit card? Would that be MasterCard, VISA, or American Express?

Verify information. Could I have your address please? (Compare with the address you have on your phone list and update it if it has changed.) Credit card number? Expiration date? I'll have your Compuday shipped out tomorrow.

Show appreciation. Great! I know you're going to find your Compuday to be a perfect organizer. And if you decide you want to order another as a gift, please be sure to ask for me so that you will receive a twenty percent discount. I'll enclose my card. Thank you for your order, *(prospect's name)*, and I look forward to talking with you again!

Although this sample script provides an overview of how a presentation might proceed, it is important to remember that each and every call is going to be slightly different. You must keep the human factor in mind and make each call feel natural.

Tip-Top Telemarketing Reps

People have their own opinions, ideas and desires. Because of this, sometimes a presentation will hit the mark and sometimes it will be way off target. Learning how to revise the presentation so it does have a positive effect most of the time comes from practice, practice, and more practice.

It is often a good idea to schedule regular role-playing, even with your experienced telemarketing reps who often get stuck in a rut or reach a point where they feel overconfident. Role-playing is best done on a one-on-one basis in front of others.

Have your most successful reps go first to show how it should be done. Have another employee play the part of the prospect and throw out objections to ensure the rep can respond logically and smoothly.

Trainees should be able to present the material with little word-for-word script reading and be able to answer objections quickly and confidently. Videotaping or audio recording a role-playing session is an excellent instructional technique.

The most profitable telemarketing-service bureau owners schedule regular sales meetings—some as often as three times a week—to keep reps on their toes. Others claim that a daily pep talk in combination with a weekly sales meeting does the trick. You will find what works through trial-and-error; the proof will be in how your reps produce.

Tools of the Trade

Your telemarketing representatives' job will be made much easier if you provide them with all of the proper support and tools. One tool that is not only convenient, but should be considered an absolute necessity, is a Sales Reference Kit that contains all the paperwork necessary to make a presentation.

There are products available that have been designed with telemarketers in mind. The Tel-Easel, for example, consists of two three-ring binders mounted on a single plexiglass easel for easy information access.

However, it is possible to develop your own Sales Reference Kits. Primarily, this is nothing more than a three-ring binder or a clipboard sectioned off to contain the following materials:

- The Telephone Sales Script
- List of Benefits
- Objections & Rebuttals
- Product Literature
- Specifications/Price List
- Other Information Sheets
- Order Forms
- Call Records & Summaries

Providing your reps with information at their fingertips will smooth the transitions in a presentation. It will help them feel more confident and sound more professional. ■

19

Overcoming Objections

A successful, confident salesperson will always consider a "No" to mean "Show Me." In fact, many people who sell for a living claim they love "No" because it gives them the opportunity to do what they do best . . . convince someone that they should have the product or service.

Objections fall into the same category. Basically, they are roadblocks put up by a potential customer for one of several reasons:

1. Requesting more information,
2. Wanting to be perfectly comfortable about parting with their hard-earned money, or
3. Making sure the product or service will complement or improve their life in some way. Of course, there are going to be occasions when someone presents objections just because they are an annoying sort of person, but those situations are rare.

Generally, objections are made in the form of a statement: "I don't need it now," "We always buy from the same company," "The price is too high." They must be acknowledged if you plan to close the sale. An unanswered objection will continue to be a roadblock, no matter how the rest of the presentation goes. Even if it seems ridiculous, it must be addressed because it is obviously an important point to the customer.

Here are a few tips to remember when faced with objections:

1. Objections often point out a problem. "The price is too high" may indicate financial problems. The telemarketer's job is to find a solution. "We have an easy 60-day payment plan," "We can finance the purchase," or "If you buy today, I can give you a twenty-five percent discount." Any of these rebuttals may set the prospective customer's mind at ease, and help close the sale.

2. Objections are often unfounded. "Maybe I'll buy one next week." The telemarketer realizes that this is strictly a roadblock and might respond, "This is a one-time offer that won't be available next week," or "I understand. I'll call you next week," or "Is there a reason why you prefer to wait until next week?"

3. Never create a disagreement. If a prospect claims they can't afford the product or service, the rep must never try to prove them wrong by telling them they *can* afford it. The best path to take is that of finding a solution.

4. Develop an objection and response list for each new telemarketing campaign. Although there are standard objections (no money, can't talk right now, don't want it, don't need it), there are going to be those which are specific to the product or service being sold. Considering all the possibilities before starting the campaign will ensure that none of the reps gets caught off guard. Even so, there may be a few surprises. Encourage reps to share new objections and the responses with their coworkers during sales meetings.

5. If you or your reps really do not know the answer to a genuine question that is raised as an objection, especially if it is technical in nature, be honest. Explain that you will get all the details and find out the best time to call back with the information so the prospective customer will be prepared to continue the conversation.

A Few Common Objections and How to Overcome Them:

1. *It's too expensive.*
   It does seem that everything is more expensive lately, that's true. However, when you consider all you get for your money, I think you'll agree that it is actually a bargain in the long run.
2. *I can't really make that decision.*
   If you give me the name of the person who does make the purchasing decisions, I can give them a call directly. Or, if you prefer, I'll call you back tomorrow so you can get the O.K. on this.
3. *I never buy anything over the telephone.*
   I can understand that. However, you in turn must understand that we are willing to send you the product and bill you for it next month. I think that indicates our willingness to trust you. Tell me, did you have a bad experience at some point?
4. *Let me think about it.*
   That's always a good idea. Are there any other questions you have? Which would be the best time for me to call you back—Tuesday at 11 a.m. or Thursday at 6 p.m.?
5. *Doesn't it come in blue?*
   Would you buy it in blue?
6. *Can you give me a discount?*
   I have already given you a discounted price. I will, however, be happy to offer you free delivery (or warranty or whatever) if you order today.
7. *We always buy from my brother-in-law.*
   It is often a good idea to deal with people you know. What are you currently paying? Are you convinced that you are getting the best possible value?
8. *I've heard that your service department is slow.*
   Let me assure you that if you ever need service, you can call me directly and I will handle it.

9. *I don't think I would like it.*
   How do you know if you would like it when you haven't even seen it?

10. *That's part of the problem. I can't see it before I buy it.*
   That would only be a problem if we didn't offer you the best 30-day money-back guarantee available. Or, if you prefer, I can hold your check for 30 days and if, during that period, you call and tell me you don't want to keep it, you can return it and I will send back your check. Now, shall I write that order up?

This listing will give you a start in creating your own objection-and-response sheet. Realizing that there are only so many objections that can be raised—although they can be presented in a hundred different ways— will give you and your telemarketing reps a basis from which to build.

Cover as many objections as possible in sales meetings and encourage everyone to make notes of new ones. Remember that the more knowledge the reps have about the product, the company and the competition, the easier it will be for them to overcome objections. ■

20

Trade Terminology

In discussion of your telemarketing tools thus far, we've made reference primarily to "equipment." That's a little too simple; there are terms and words which are unique to the industry. It's never too early to learn the lingo of your business. While you're getting started, keep some of these more common terms in mind:

Bird-Dogging. Finding prospective customers by asking current clients for referrals.

Burnout. Exhaustion or lack of motivation caused by overwork, low pay, poor supervision, lack of training, etc.

Buzz Words. Descriptive adverbs and adjectives that make a sales presentation exciting.

Canned Call. Following a script word-for-word. Usually works best with surveys and other information-gathering processes.

Closing. Asking the prospective customer for an order.

Cold Call. Talking with prospective customers who have little or no knowledge of the product or company.

Cross Directory. A telephone directory that is arranged by street addresses followed by name and phone number. Also known as a criss-cross directory.

Data Processing. Maintenance of data—generally computerized—for the purpose of analysis, storage, sorting and upgrading. Used in telemarketing to keep track of lists, orders, call records and results.

Decision Maker. The person who can make the decision to buy the product or service being promoted.

Demographic. Describes various statistics of a population, including occupation, address, age, sex, number of children, hobbies, etc. Valuable when renting or examining lists to determine if a specific group will be a viable market for a product or service.

Direct Mail. A marketing campaign that involves sending a brochure or other promotional literature through the mail. Often used in conjunction with telemarketing.

Follow-Up. The term used to describe scheduled calling to confirm receipt of an order or sales literature, promote a new product, or gather survey information about service.

Fulfillment. The actual filling and shipping of an order.

Hot Lead. The name and telephone number of a qualified prospect.

Inbound. Incoming calls, generally part of a customer service program utilizing a toll-free 800 number.

List Brokerage. A company that maintains and rents lists or directories of prospective customers. Lists are available in hundreds of demographic categories, including age, occupation, income, hobbies, homeowner or renter, number of children, etc.

Long Distance Carrier. An independent telephone company that strictly handles and controls long distance calls.

Monitor. The ability, via three-way calling or special monitoring equipment, to listen to telemarketing representatives without interrupting their conversation. Can be done with or without their knowledge as a training tool or to check up on their presentations.

Objection. An argument, disagreement or misunderstanding that a prospective customer introduces during a sales presentation. Must be overcome to ensure getting a sale or any other expected result.

Qualified Lead or Qualified Prospect. The name of a person who has been identified as being capable of or interested in buying a service or product. This can include being the decision maker, having a good credit rating, or being a satisfied past customer.

Sales Call Report. An easy-to-follow form that summarizes a telemarketing rep's daily or weekly calling activity.

Sales Reference Kit. A three-ring binder or clipboard that contains all of the literature and paperwork needed by a telemarketing rep to make their presentation.

Script. A prepared manuscript developed for telemarketing reps to follow while giving a presentation.

Toll-Free 800. A telephone service that is used to encourage inbound calling for products and services. Offers low-cost customer service and is available through most long-distance carriers.

WATS (Wide Area Telecommunication Service). Long distance calling service that provides discounts according to distance and time of a call. Available through most long-distance carriers.

As you run across more industry "lingo," find out what it means and make note of the new terminology below. ■

_____

_____

_____

_____

_____

_____

_____

_____

Notes

Key Points

_____

_____

_____

Personal Thoughts

_____

_____

_____

_____

_____

Additional Research

_____

_____

_____

_____

_____

21

Hiring Employees

You may decide to handle your first accounts yourself, especially if you are starting small. Even so, it won't take long to realize that some help will make the work go a lot more smoothly and will also increase your potential to realize big profits.

You can start with part-time employees who work on an as-needed basis. If possible, hire them as independent contractors, which means they take care of their own insurance and taxes. This saves you money and time.

You simply pay a small hourly wage (minimum of $4.50 and up to $10 per hour) plus a commission (two to twenty percent depending on the area of the country and the product being sold) per sale or, in the case of creating leads or conducting surveys, a fee (generally $2 to $5) for each bona fide lead or completed series of questions. There are, of course, variables you may wish to employ based on each project.

Knowledge is of two kinds.
We know a subject ourselves or we know
where we can find information on it.

Samuel Johnson

Once you get a full-scale telemarketing service bureau going, you can figure on creating staff positions and titles to ensure smooth operation of your business. Telemarketing

A Few Ideas for Productivity Bonuses

- *Cash Award*
- *Dinner for Two*
- *A Day Off with Pay*
- *Paid Weekend Vacation*
- *Night on the Town*
- *Two Days Off with Pay*
- *Compact Camera*
- *Gift Certificate*

success is dependent on supportive management and experienced trainers, which leads to happy and enthusiastic representatives. The most common job titles within service bureaus, and the responsibilities connected with each, are as follows:

Director.   Oversees the total operation, including planning and implementing telemarketing programs for clients, monitoring profitability, determining pricing, selecting equipment, designing work stations, developing an operating budget, and working with clients in a public-relations capacity.

Sales Executive.   Responsible for marketing and selling telemarketing services to prospective clients, working closely with director and manager in developing services that meet client needs, developing campaigns for individual clients, promoting new programs, and creating advertising and promotional materials to recruit and maintain business accounts.

Manager.   Responsible for the smooth operation of the service bureau, including working with the director on program development and implementation; scheduling of employees and design of shifts; overall management of projects including client liaison, billing, and reports; working on the generation of prospective client leads for telemarketing representatives; and maintenance of equipment.

Supervisor. Responsible for hiring and training of telemarketing representatives, assigning them to projects and shifts, handling distribution of leads, managing employees in a supportive fashion with pep talks and sales meetings, preparing goals and daily, weekly, and monthly summaries of projects. Works closely with trainer (see below) or sometimes incorporates trainer's responsibilities into this job description, depending on budget and size of operation.

Trainer. Hires employees, maintains employee records, develops and implements training manual, monitors reps, conducts regular sales meetings, pep talks and workshops to cover new technology or selling methods, establishes telemarketing standards and works closely with manager and supervisor on developing telemarketing scripts for individual projects.

Telemarketing Representative. The front line, so to speak, of the operation, reps are the ones who must communicate and sell the product or service to customers, maintain accurate records of calls, sales and other information required by management, maintain a high level of product knowledge, and promote the integrity of the telemarketing service bureau by being enthusiastic, polite, and professional.

In terms of how many reps you will need, most bureaus figure that one good rep should be able to make a minimum of ten calls per hour based on a tight, specific script and a relatively "easy-selling" product or service. The estimated results of individual telemarketing jobs, e.g., 300 calls per day or fifteen completed surveys per hour, will also dictate how many reps you need at any given time.

Of course, every assignment will have the following variables:

- How many calls the reps are expected to make in order to try to reach the party.
- Whether they must get through a front line of secretaries and middle management personnel to reach a decision maker.
- How recently the telephone number listing has been updated to reduce the incidence of wrong or disconnected numbers.
- The complexity of the product or service being sold or promoted.
- The experience of the reps; their ability to maintain control of the conversation and to know exactly when to move in for a close.

You can find your own employees through ads in the classified section of the local paper, listings with college and university student employment offices (many schools have Marketing and Advertising courses—a perfect group of students for your part-time needs), or by word-of-mouth.

Another option is to sign on with a temporary help agency. The agency will take care of all the screening and initial interviewing for you and then send you the most qualified people. For this service, they will charge you a fee per hour for every person you use. Obviously, it is less expensive to hire your employees rather than have an agency recruit them. The other advantage to doing your own screening is that you can hire the people you think will best fit in on the specific jobs, you will know what to expect from them, and also can personally train employees who work for you on any kind of regular basis. With the agency, you may be at their mercy and required to take whoever they can manage to find for your job.

Your employees are representatives of your business, so they should be polite, efficient and professional. Although the people they are talking to never see them, it is proven that reps who get dressed for the job are more confident and comfortable. Discourage sloppy clothes and work habits. Your reputation is in the hands, so to speak, of those working on a job, so be sure they are the kind of people you would imagine yourself spending time talking to—and buying from—on the telephone.

Special Qualifications for Telemarketers

The first rule to remember when interviewing and hiring telemarketing representatives is that a sales background does *not* always mean a person can be successful when working only with a telephone. Although your employees must have basic sales skill, there is more to it than that.

For example, in regular sales, a salesperson can create a visual impression and spend a little time getting to know the prospective client, even stopping by to chat several times before trying to close the sale. In telemarketing, your reps have one chance to make a positive impression and it's all dependent on their tone of voice. Here are some other aspects of telephone sales that must be kept in mind when interviewing prospective employees:

1. Reps must have clear, upbeat speaking voices that are pleasant to the ear. The first contact they have with a prospective customer is "Hello, this is Mary (or Bob) from ABC and I'm calling to speak with ..." If they sound cheerful, yet professional, and speak distinctly rather than slurring words and phrases, it greatly improves their chances of completing the call satisfactorily.
2. The rate of rejection in telephone sales is appreciably higher than in most other sales situations; some say as high as ninety percent rejection. Your reps must have a positive

attitude, the ability to realize that a rejection is never personally directed at them and a basically cheerful disposition that will carry them through from sale to sale.

3. Your reps must be thoughtful and considerate of the customers' needs. Often, seemingly silly questions or comments are just a potential buyer's way of saying, "Convince me I need this item."

   Listening not only to what is being said but *how* it is being said can give a rep insights on attitudes, problems and buying signals. Getting impatient or angry at indecision could mean a lost sale and, overall, an ineffective telemarketer.

4. A person who is quick and organized is sure to do well in this business. Every objection under the sun is going to be thrown out at some point and reps must have the comebacks at the tip of their tongue. They need to be aware of all features and benefits of the product or service they are selling, including prices, warranties, color, sizes, and shipping information.

5. Self-motivation is a big plus. There will be times when hours go by without a sale. The rep who can still pick up the phone and make another call is the one who will be successful. Selling can be a lonely job. You want people with the ability to keep going over the long haul, realizing that the very next call could mean a major sale.

6. The telemarketing crew represents you and your business. Therefore, you want employees who are ethical; presenting honest information about the products or services being sold; recognizing the necessity of creating long-term goodwill with customers rather than going for the quick sale; exhibiting sincerity about the benefits to the customer. You definitely do not want telemarketing reps who are rude, dishonest, drunk, or grouchy. This is where a monitoring feature on your telephone system comes in handy; you can spot-check the performance of any rep at any time.

The Employment Interview

Even before you get to the actual interview process with candidates, you have a perfect opportunity to develop a feeling about their potential. Put a telephone number in the employment ad and have them call you. You can then make an evaluation about the tone of voice, diction, and how enthusiastic and positive they sound on the telephone. At this point, they are trying to sell you on their ability to do the job . . . if they fail at this step, you can be pretty sure they won't make it under pressure.

However, if you get a sense that they are capable of projecting the image you want over the telephone, definitely set up an appointment to meet them in person. This is when you try to determine whether or not they will fit in with the rest of your crew as a team player, whether they truly understand the principles behind telemarketing, and if they seem to have the qualities the job requires.

Asking the recruit personal questions (not too personal, however, such as anything related to age, religion, marital status, and anything else that might be considered discriminatory) about their favorite job, least favorite job, educational background, why they think they would be successful in telemarketing, etc., will show you whether they can think fast.

Throwing them a curve, such as having them tell you about a movie or book they loved, will also be a good indicator of response and enthusiasm. As a final test, you may even consider doing a bit of role-playing. Set the recruit up at a telephone extension in an adjoining room and give them five minutes to review a prepared script on a fictitious product. Then, have them call you on the extension and make an actual presentation. Explain to them that you realize this is spur-of-the-moment and is not meant to intimidate them.

The truth of the matter, however, is that if they fail miserably in making even an attempt at a presentation, if they squirm at simple objections you bring up and seem unable to respond, you probably wouldn't have much success in training them. If they've got it, they've got it and you should hire them immediately. If they don't, you're going to be investing a great deal of time and energy on a big gamble.

Someone with the basics—enthusiasm, a good phone voice, sincerity, positive attitude, willingness to listen, and quick-thinking—has the potential to become a valuable part of your operation.

If you train and manage properly, (using role-playing and videotaping, offering constructive critiques of presentations, creating healthy competition between reps, awarding bonuses for the most sales or some other achievement), and encourage open communication within the work space, it is guaranteed that you will have a productive staff of dedicated, happy employees.

Telemarketing Guidelines

- Never chew gum or eat while on a call.
- Smile as you speak—the prospect will hear it in your voice.
- Do not swear or raise your voice on the phone.
- Speak clearly; do not slur your words.
- No matter what, never hang up on a prospect.
- Answer all objections directly and honestly.
- Never assume to know what a prospect wants or needs. If it isn't clear, ask.
- Be friendly, but don't joke. A sense of humor is a very personal matter and it could get you into trouble if it isn't in line with what the prospect finds funny.
- Always be polite, even if the prospect doesn't extend the same courtesy.
- If tired or in a bad mood, don't make calls until you are feeling positive and/or refreshed. Any negativity or

grogginess will come across as being unenthusiastic and uninteresting.

- Listen to what prospects have has to say and always acknowledge their opinions before offering a rebuttal to their objection. Careful listening will give you clues as to their needs, desires, and concerns.
- Complete all steps connected with a call—filling out order forms, shipping information, call record, etc.—before moving on to the next prospect call.
- Do not push or harass the prospect into a sale. They will probably cancel anyway, as well as getting a very bad taste for telemarketing.
- Never argue or debate with a prospective customer.
- Never lie, exaggerate or misrepresent the product, service or company you are promoting.
- Know the product and understand its capabilities and features to ensure confidence and professionalism. ■

Notes

Key Points

_____

_____

_____

Personal Thoughts

_____

_____

_____

_____

_____

Additional Research

_____

_____

_____

_____

_____

22

Advertising Your Business

More than 150 years ago, Thomas Macaulay, a British historian and statesman, said, "Advertising is to business what steam is to industry. [They provide] the same propelling power."

Few in business would argue with Macaulay's observation — it is as true today as it was when steam was the driving force behind industry. But the question remains, "How do you get the most out of your advertising dollar?" The answer is to:

1. Know your customer,
2. Target your market, and
3. Understand the basics of advertising.

In this chapter, we will provide an overview of various aspects of advertising, including how to use circulation figures to figure your Cost Per Thousand (CPM) and how to create ads that will bring results.

What is Advertising?

Advertising informs the public about:

- Who you are,
- What kind of business you operate,
- How they can buy your products or services, and
- Why they should come to you.

Before you even open the doors of your business, you should start thinking about your advertising program—how much money you can afford to spend, where your dollars will be best spent, and how to structure your campaign.

Decide what kind of results you expect. Are you looking for immediate sales or on-going recognition? What kind of customers are you hoping to attract? Are you emphasizing price, service, workmanship, or something unique? Once you have answered these questions, your decision as to the best type of advertising for the allotted dollars will be easier to make.

There are three basic types of advertising that you will be most interested in during the first few years of your business.

Start-up advertising. This includes your business cards and stationery, the flyers and brochures you have created to pass out around the neighborhood announcing your new business, and your initial newspaper advertising campaign. At this point, your main focus will be on telling people where you are located and what you can offer them.

Ongoing advertising. Once the business is "up and running," so to speak, it will be vital to your success to institute a regular advertising campaign that is well-planned and consistent. Your goal, at this point, is to maintain your established customers, increase your market base, introduce new products or services and promote sales to clear inventory or encourage new clients to use your service.

Looking good. After you have reached the point where your business is on steady ground and showing increased profits every year, you can afford to dabble in "institutional advertising," as it is called in the trade. This is where you pick up the tab to send a dozen kids to the rodeo when it comes to town, or sponsor a float in the local Fourth of July parade and, in return, get your name listed on the program or on a banner in the parade. This is primarily name recognition only and, while every little bit is helpful, by the time you can afford it, you probably will be in pretty good shape anyway.

Advertising Your Telemarketing Services

The big profits in telemarketing come from the few good corporate accounts that utilize your services on a regular basis. Although you can certainly make a living with only doctors, lawyers, and small business owners as clients, corporations have the need—and the money—for telemarketing on both an inbound and an outbound basis to handle everything from order-taking and customer service to surveys and follow-up public relations calls.

There are several ways to reach the clientele you want to attract. First of all, it is imperative that you put an ad in the Yellow Pages for your area. The Yellow Pages are often the first place a potential client will look when in the market for a particular service or product. Applying for your business phone entitles you to one free listing in the category of your choice.

Supplemental listings cost extra and a display ad can run anywhere from $50 to $1,000 per month, depending on the size of the area being served and specific directory rates. You should also check what it would cost for you to run a listing in the Yellow Pages of nearby cities—undoubtedly home to some large corporations, or at least branch offices of major companies that would benefit from your services.

This may be one of the most effective uses of your advertising budget, especially for your telemarketing business. Some business owners, in fact, count on Yellow Page advertising to such a great extent that they plan their company name around it—Aardvark Plumbing or AAA Telecommunications —just to ensure top billing in their specific category.

One thing to be aware of is that phone directories are published once a year. So, if you are planning on capturing a

Yellow Page audience, check with the directory sales department for deadlines on inserting ads in your regional phone book. The number is listed in the front of the directory.

Appealing to Industry Leaders

An excellent way to recruit business is to run classified and display ads in trade publications and business magazines. As an example, if you decided that you wanted to work primarily with insurance companies, an ad in *Insurance Review* magazine or any other industry tabloid listed in the Standard Rate & Data Service (SRDS) or the Directory of Newsletters (both available through the library) would be a good idea.

The same principle would apply if your desired clientele were doctors, lawyers, or oil companies—check the SRDS and the Directory for publications specifically written for the medical, legal and/or petroleum industries and call or write requesting a media kit, which outlines a publication's circulation, ad sizes and mechanical requirements, general editorial focus, audience overview, and advertising rates.

Classified Advertising

Don't underestimate the power of classified ads. Many major corporations utilize the classifieds even though they have sizable budgets available for display advertising. There are several reasons for this:

1. The classifieds are an extremely reliable testing ground for new products, services, and ideas. Although it is true that people who typically "read" the classifieds are a different group from those who scan display ads, they are considered to be responsive and, therefore, can give you a very good idea of whether or not you have placed your ad in the appropriate publication.

2. A short, well-written classified placed in the right publication and under the proper category can be a low-cost method of advertising guaranteeing solid returns.

3. If a company is trying to establish a mailing list for follow-up mailings of special products and other offers, a classified ad that features an "Inquiry" statement, such as "Send name & address for free details," is a good way to build up a file of qualified buyer's names. And they can be considered qualified buyers because it takes time, energy and the cost of a postage stamp for them to get your free information. By writing to you they have stated their interest.

4. Classified ads are inexpensive, ranging from 50 cents to $15 per word depending on the publication. With careful planning, you should be able to get broad-based coverage without putting a dent in your operating capital.

When writing a classified ad it's necessary to get as much information in as small a space as possible. Since there is usually no art and your ad will be surrounded by many others, you must catch the reader's eye with the first few words. Therefore, you must make them as exciting as possible.

Use persuasion words in your ad which grab the reader's attention. Powerful persuaders include such words as *save, earn, free, secret, learn, how-to, success, results* or *power*. There are others which you will pick up by studying the classifieds.

It always helps to capitalize these lead words or to have them set in **bold type**. Some newspapers and magazines offer large check marks, stars, or other grabbers to incorporate into the ad for a small charge.

Display Advertising

As with classified advertising, when you consider running a display ad, it is important to define your market, select a publication that will reach the audience you want, and create an ad that appeals specifically to them.

The drawback of display ads is that they are significantly more expensive than classifieds. But inserted in the right publication, they can pull a tremendous response.

If there are magazines you're interested in for display space, find the advertising representative's name in the editorial box (generally on one of the first few pages in the magazine) and write for a rate card.

Advertising is the greatest art form of the 20th Century.

Marshall McLuhan

And remember: Whether classified or display, *always test an ad* before using it heavily. Test it in different publications, as a direct-mail insert, and/or on a self-mailer. It's better to begin with one small ad or area and record your responses accurately. Then by projecting the percentage of responses to the number of people who were exposed to the ad, determine how many people would be likely to respond if you reached a greater number of possible customers.

If you receive a disappointing few, you'll know you need to change your ad—without having spent a lot of money on advertising. If you receive an overwhelming response, you can handle a smaller number more easily and have satisfied customers. If you "go for it" and receive too many orders at first, you may well find yourself unable to fill them.

One important note on classified and display advertising: When you find an ad that works, stick with it. You've heard the line about duplicating your past successes. Advertising is the same. Although you may want to upgrade or experiment a bit, once you have a winner which appeals to the needs of readers and results in steady clients, work within the prototype. It definitely pays to repeat a good thing.

Writing display ad copy is not for the inexperienced. Although it is possible to learn how to put ideas and words together that will pull the results you desire, it is recommended that you hire a copywriter if you have any qualms about producing an ad.

If you are confident that you can develop your own ad, remember that it must build identity through the use of carefully planned words and design. Glance through newspapers and magazines to find ads that catch your eye. Most likely, the ones that stand out have a memorable logo, effective use of space which carries your eye to a significant point or an unusual headline that leads you into the body of the ad. These are the ads you should refer to as samples when designing your own. When planning your ad, keep the following elements in mind:

1. *Visibility.* Your ad may well be surrounded by many others, so you must design it to attract the reader's attention.
2. *Boldness.* Use large art and/or a bold headline as a focal point.
3. *Simplicity.* Don't overwhelm the reader with too many fine details. This is the general rule of thumb. However, many mail order experts claim the more copy in the ad, the greater the response. The feeling is that the reader gets a chance to learn so much more about your product, as well as discovering something about the supplier. This makes them feel comfortable about committing to order.
4. *White space.* Just because you have, say, a 4 x 6-inch space to work with, it isn't necessary to fill it up with graphics. In fact, white space is a necessary component in assuring your ad will be read.

5. *Use legible typefaces.* The easiest to read are Times Roman and Palatino (the type used in this book), which are known as serif typefaces because of the tiny strokes at the tops and bottoms of the letters. Sanserif (without strokes) types such as Helvetica are O.K. for ads containing few words, but are difficult for the eye to follow when there is a lot of text. Also, be sure that the type is large enough; generally nothing smaller than a 10-point type should be used.

Design and Typesetting

It isn't necessary to be a great artist to create an ad, especially these days with the availability of impressive graphic materials, including cut-out and transfer (press-on) letters in different typefaces, symbols, borders, and designs (available through graphic art supply companies), such as Formatt and Chartpak. Also, most word processors have computer graphics available that can really dress up your ad at a low cost.

If you feel uncomfortable about laying out your ad so that it has eye appeal, consider hiring an art student to handle the job for a prearranged fee or as a school assignment (talk with the head of the art department to see if they have a work/study for credit program). Just be sure to review the student's work prior to making a commitment.

Also, check with the advertising department of the newspaper or magazine you are planning to advertise in. There may be graphic artists or designers on staff who will work on the layout for you. In fact, there still are newspapers in the country that offer full services, from ad concept to design work, at a minimal charge to their advertising clients.

Publications work on tight deadlines so be sure you start the process early enough to get a proof copy of your ad back in time to make any corrections. You can imagine the anguish in seeing your ad appear—with the wrong address. Although the publication would probably do a "make-good" for you and run a corrected ad at no charge, the damage has already been done. The final responsibility for the ad rests on you, so as with any other aspect of your business, plan ahead.

There is a standardized formula in advertising which provides a barometer for predicting how much response can be expected from either a display or classified ad. The formula states that you will see 1/2 of the total responses from an ad within a certain period of time after receiving your first inquiry or order.

For an ad run in a daily newspaper, the period of time is three days; for a weekly newspaper or magazine, it is six days; within 15 days for a monthly publication, and within 25 days when running in a bi-monthly. Although there will be exceptions to this rule, it does give you a base from which to track response.

Cost Per Thousand (CPM)

The CPM equation helps you develop a cost-effective campaign. Basically, it tells you what your ad cost per 1,000 readers will be. Most publications will provide a CPM comparison upon request (some include it in their Media Kits), but you can easily figure it out for yourself with just a few facts from publications you are exploring as advertising vehicles.

For convenience sake, CPM equations are typically based on the rate of a full-page black and white ad. You simply divide the full-page rate by the thousands of circulation. And it is important that you get the circulation, *not* the readership, for magazines and newspapers typically claim that their readership is two to fifty percent higher because of "pass-along" of the publication to friends or relatives.

For example, if a certain newspaper is charging $2,000 for a full-page ad and they claim their true circulation is 200,000, you will be paying $10 per 1,000 readers for your ad space. Another specialized publication's full-page rate may be $1,000 with a circulation of 50,000. The cost per 1,000 readers will be much higher— $20 per 1,000, but it might be worth it if, for example, you have a unique product or service that is geared to an exclusive market.

Benefits of Paid Circulation

It is also important to know that publications with a paid circulation generally have a readership that is more inclined to respond to advertising. This is because of the simple fact that they are a captive audience who have taken the time to *order* the publication. This is especially valuable if you have a product or service that you are planning to market through mail order channels.

You can find circulation, readership demographics, advertising rates and other important information about a number of publications (especially those with national distribution) through Standard Rate and Data (SR&D) or the Gale Directory of Publications (and their monthly updates), available through the research desk at your local library.

Recently, the Advertising Research Foundation and the Association of Business Publishers conducted a study to determine the effects of advertising on the sale of products.

Several different products were used for the study and each was advertised for a 12-month period in an appropriate publication. The results were interesting, but not surprising to anyone who has ever utilized a solid advertising campaign in promoting their business.

- More advertising meant more sales.
- Increased exposure meant increased sales leads.
- Determining results from an advertising campaign generally took four to six months. One or two insertions did not indicate viable results.

- Color in ads dramatically increased response and sales.
- A well-developed ad campaign keeps on working for a year and sometimes even longer in publications with a high "keep" appeal.

The AIDA Principle

AIDA is the long established rule of thumb to follow when writing your ad copy.

AIDA *stands for Attention, Interest, Desire and Action. This means you must get the readers'* **attention** *with an eye-catching headline, keep their* **interest** *with a secondary phrase that expands on the main thought, create* **desire** *by indicating the benefits the reader will enjoy by buying your product or using your service, and, finally, encourage* **action** *by inviting them to visit or call for details on how they can realize the benefits.*

Predicting Response

All of the methods outlined above, along with others you will develop, keep your name in the consumer's mind. The effectiveness of an advertising and/or publicity campaign can be measured by conducting a simple marketing survey with new customers. Simply make it standard practice to ask them where they heard about you and your business.

Keep a tally of the responses in a notebook. A periodic review will give you hints of where to allocate future advertising funds. If, for example, the majority of your customers are being drawn from your display ad in the local newspaper, keep it going on a steady basis. If, however, you discover that most of your business is from personal contact or word-of-mouth referrals, you should concentrate on boosting your promotional efforts.

A Case for Direct Mail

Another aspect of the telemarketing business is direct mail—both from the standpoint of recruiting business and as a service you may want to consider offering your clients at some point.

The phrase may not mean much to you at this point, but as you progress in telemarketing it will mean more, since the two often go hand-in-hand. You get direct mail pieces all the time: those catalogs, brochures or other solicitation materials you receive in the mail almost daily from people you've never contacted? That's direct mail.

Since you haven't requested this information, you may throw it away without a second glance. However, if it's an attractive or unusual advertising piece, you might decide to look it over. Maybe something—a picture or catchy copy—grabs your eye and you order a product from the company that mailed the material—either by mailing in an enclosed order form or calling the listed toll-free 800 number provided (the telemarketing tie-in).

This is one example of direct mail; unsolicited advertising material which is mailed out to a large group of people. The addressees may be bound by any number of factors—they may all be credit card holders, members of an organization, the same ethnic group, age, occupation. Or they may all simply have the same zip code.

These and the names of people in thousands of other categories—hobbies, number of children, income, subscribing to the same magazines, buying items over the telephone or voting for the same candidate—are accumulated, organized and sold (or, as it is known in the business, rented) by mailing-list brokers for use in direct mail and telemarketing campaigns.

There are advantages to using direct mail when starting out, despite the cost, which can run from $65 and up per thousand names. The primary benefit is control. You can rent a mailing list that is made up of the names, addresses and, in many cases, the telephone numbers of very specific groups of people. There are two distinct uses of mailing lists for telemarketers:

1. As a way of generating leads for your clients, and
2. To help you promote your service (by renting lists of small business owners in your state, for example).

Mailing lists can be compiled by you as you gather names, or you can rent/buy them from a list broker. Check in the library for a *Direct Mail Standard Rate and Data Service (SRDS)* volume or through one of the direct marketing associations listed in the Resources chapter of this book to find brokers in the areas you desire.

The list broker is paid a commission on each rental by the owner of the list, which might be based on a magazine's subscribers, the names of people who have purchased items through certain catalogs or hundreds of possibilities. The broker will help you find the lists that most closely match the kinds of people you need to reach to satisfy your telemarketing client's objectives. And if there isn't a specific list available, the list broker can work on creating one for you.

Or, if you find a list that provides the names and addresses of a perfect target group, but no telephone numbers, you can compile them yourself using telephone books, street cross directories or by calling directory assistance. In addition, there are companies that specialize in finding telephone numbers to add to existing lists—check your Yellow Pages under research and direct market support services.

You may not even need a rental list. The phone book is an excellent resource for compiling a mailing list. If you want to focus on telemarketing for insurance companies, for example, look in the Yellow Pages and make a list of all the agencies, brokers and individual agents you'd like to approach. Do the same with any other segment of the population or business world.

A solid telemarketing/direct mail campaign to try and secure new clients for your telemarketing bureau would go something like this: First, you would call the company you were interested in approaching, find out who the main decision-maker would be and, if possible, introduce yourself and advise him or her that a letter outlining your service was on the way. When the letter is actually en route to the proper party, give it a few days and then call back to be sure it arrived safely and to see if there are further questions or the possibility of setting up an appointment.

You want a letter that is both a handshake to introduce yourself and a sales pitch. It can be a tough balance. Sales letters are the least expensive direct mail pieces to produce, but they are far from the easiest to write. You may want to hire a copywriter to handle the task, for best results.

If you choose to write the letter yourself, bear in mind these points:

- The letter is an introduction to potential buyers.
- It must have a dynamic lead-in sentence.
- It must present crisp and clear information about the benefits of dealing with you rather than your competition.
- It must present a feeling of personal communication, written just for the person who's reading it.
- It must be highly professional.

Think of what it takes to draw you into a direct mail piece and keep you interested until the last word: a thought-provoking phrase in big, bold letters at the top of the page; a simple but thorough explanation of why the letter is being sent and how reading it will be of benefit to you; a direct request to take action; a few testimonials from current service users; the signature of the company's president. All these factors should be considered.

Experiment with writing a letter, get some feedback from friends and associates—perhaps even test it locally—but make sure you're sending out something you *truly* think will work for you. Include your name and phone number in case the potential client can't wait to talk to you. If handled effectively, the combination of direct mail and phone follow-up can generate a great deal of business. ■

Notes

Key Points

_____

_____

_____

_____

Personal Thoughts

_____

_____

_____

_____

_____

_____

Additional Research

_____

_____

_____

_____

_____

23

Promotion and Public Relations

Informing the public about your business through the use of business cards, brochures, mailing pieces, catalogs and specialty items, such as calendars, pens and T-shirts imprinted with your company name, is known as *promotion.*

The things you can do over and above your paid advertising and promotion that help build your image and keep your business in the public consciousness are referred to as *public relations.*

The words cover a lot of ground. Some businesses promote by trying to make themselves more visible. An example of this would be the new fried chicken restaurant that has someone in a chicken suit parade all day in front of the store to draw in customers. Other businesses give away premiums to increase the customer's sense of getting a good deal.

Getting into Print and Television

Publicity is another way to get attention, though you won't find "free ads." To get media publicity—mentions in newspapers, magazines, on radio or television—you need to approach outlets not as someone trying to sell services, but rather as a source of information that will benefit that medium's readers/ viewers/listeners.

Many publications have new business sections, for example. Or you might be able to get mention as a unique business in certain publications. But rarely, if ever, will you find the opportunity to sell through free publicity, because editors will see through any efforts to advertise in a press release.

Should you decide to write up a press release and do a targeted publicity mailing, bear in mind that there are four main reasons why editors throw away releases:

1. Some releases are just hype, thinly disguised commercial advertising, offering no news or information of value to the editor and his or her audience.
2. Some releases are adequate enough in their content and writing, but are sent to inappropriate prospects or sent at the wrong times.
3. Some releases are scheduled for use but get bumped when something deemed more important comes along.
4. Seasonal material must go out at the right time; remember that most publications work months ahead. If a seasonal release is received at the wrong time, it will be trashed.

The Bottom Line

The justification for investing in advertising and promotion is time. If you attempted to contact all of the people who read ads and press release material in newspapers or those who listen to talk shows, you would never have time to conduct your business—you would be too busy recruiting.

Time is money! As a small business owner, you will want to devote as much attention as possible to the production end of your venture and let your advertising and promotion work to bring in the customers.

Knowledge and belief in your product, faith in yourself and respect for your customers are the keys to succesfully building your future. As you go about starting-up and establishing your business, remember the word "profit." This alone should give you the necessary motivation to get out there and confidently tell the world what you have to offer. ◼

Notes

Key Points

_____

_____

_____

Personal Thoughts

_____

_____

_____

_____

_____

Additional Research

_____

_____

_____

_____

24

Resources

Telemarketing Information

American Management Association
135 West 50th Street
New York, NY 10020
212-586-8100

American Marketing Association
250 South Wacker Drive
Chicago, IL 60606–5819
312-648-0536

American Telemarketing Association
5000 Van Nuys Boulevard # 400
Sherman Oaks, CA 91403
818–995–7338

Direct Marketing Association
6 East 43rd Street
New York, NY 10017
212-689-4977

Direct Marketing Magazine
224 Seventh Street
Garden City, NY 11530
516-746-6700

North American Telecommunications Association
200 M Street NW
Washington, DC 20036

Telemarketing Magazine
1 Technology Plaza
Norwalk, CT 06854
800-243-6002

Telemarketing Managers Association
3100 West Lake Street
Minneapolis, MN 55416
612-927-9220

List Brokers & Sources

Standard Rate & Data Service
5201 Old Orchard Road
Skokie, IL 60077
(Check your local library for the Direct Mail List
Rates & Data)

American Direct Marketing Services
1261 Record Crossing
Dallas, TX 75235
800-527-5080

R. L. Polk & Co.
4850 Baumgartner Road
St. Louis, MO 43129
314-894-3590

Market Data Retrieval
16 Progress Drive
Shelton, CT 06484
800–243–5538

Metromail
901 West Bond Street
Lincoln, NE 68521–3694
800–228–4571

Publications

Sales and Marketing Management Magazine, 633 Third Ave., New York, NY 10022.

General Reference Books & Periodicals

A Consumer's Guide to Telephone Service. Consumer Information Center, Pueblo, CO 81009.

Bacon's Publicity Checker. R. H. Bacon and Company, Chicago, IL. (A comprehensive listing of major newspapers in the United States and Canada.)

Brownstone, David M., and Gorton Carruth. *Where to Find Business Information.* New York, NY. Wiley-Interscience, 1982.

Encyclopedia of Business Information Sources. Gale Resource Company, Detroit, MI.

National Five-Digit Zip code and Post Office Directory. U.S. Postal Service, Address Information Systems Division, 6060 Primacy Parkway, Memphis, TN 38188. (Can be ordered by telephone: call 1–800–238–3150.)

National Trade and Professional Associations of the United States. Columbia Books, Inc., Washington, DC.

Roget's International Thesaurus. New York, NY. Harper & Row, 1977.

Tax Guide for Small Businesses. Internal Revenue Service, Washington, DC. (Available through your local I. R. S. office; request publication 334.)

Ulrich's International Periodicals Directory. R. R. Bowker and Company, New York, NY.

Webster's Ninth New Collegiate Dictionary. Springfield, MA. Merriam-Webster Inc., 1983.

Small Business Associations & Government Agencies

American Marketing Association, 250 South Wacker Drive, Chicago, IL 60606-5819 (Marketing publications available to non-members).

The Association for Electronic Cottagers, P.O. Box 1738, Davis, CA 95617.

Bureau of the Census, Washington, DC 20233 (Statistical data).

Copyright Office, Library of Congress, 101 Independence Ave. SE, Washington, DC 20559 (Information on copyrighting written and visual materials).

Council of Better Business Bureaus, 1515 Wilson Blvd., Arlington, VA 22209 (Ask for a listing of their "Booklets on Wise Buying").

The Dun & Bradstreet Corporation, 299 Park Avenue, New York, NY 10171.

International Franchise Association, 1350 New York Ave. NW, Ste 900, Washington, DC 20005 (Regulation and information on franchises).

Minority Business Development Agency, Office of Public Affairs, Department of Commerce, Washington, DC 20230.

National Association for the Self-Employed, 2324 Gravel Road, Fort Worth, TX 76118.

National Association of Women Business Owners, 600 South Federal St., Ste 400, Chicago, IL 60605.

National Federation of Independent Business, 150 West 20th Ave. San Mateo, CA 94403.

National Insurance Consumers Organization, 344 Commerce Street, Alexandria, VA 22314 (Send self-addressed stamped envelope for free booklet, "Buyer's Guide to Insurance").

National Minority Business Council, Inc., 235 East 42 St., New York, NY 10017 (Quarterly newsletter for small and minority businesses).

National Small Business United, 1155 15th St. NW, Washington, DC 20005 (Send for info on federal legislation for small businesses).

National Trade and Professional Associations of the United States, available through the research desk at your local library.

Occupational Safety and Health Administration (OSHA), Department of Labor, Washington, DC 20210 (Employment regulations).

Office of Information and Public Affairs, U.S. Department of Labor, 200 Constitution Ave. NW, Washington, DC 20210 (Request publications list regarding employment).

Patent and Trademark Office, Commissioner, Washington, DC 20231 (Details on applying for a patent).

Small Business Administration, 1441 L Street NW, Washington, DC 20416 (For booklets and information on the Service Corps of Retired Executives—SCORE). ■

Index